Captain Matt's
Nonsense Chants and Silly Stories

ISBN: 979-11-982546-4-1

i

This book was made from the contents of the textbooks my wife Michelle and I developed to teach students in the modest private ESL tutoring school we run in South Korea. It came about because the English phonics books we used just couldn't seem to keep the students' attention. They do seem a bit more focused with this content, so we thought we'd see if anyone else likes it. Some of the words might seem a bit odd, but the intention is to help kids learn about putting sounds together more than gain vocabulary.

We chose to use Magic E despite its shortcomings because the Split Digraphs just don't hold a crowd. Our Magic E rule for this book is just that it must be last in line, but we know the preciseness of baseball players tells us that is not the rule, and their ties and toes and knees and even Mae's sundaes give us a clue that Magic E is not even bound to the long vowel sound in split digraph form.

But what can we say? Magic E is just more fun.

We do also accept that there are a few other slightly controversial approaches besides vocabulary and Magic E, but we hope you will allow us some artistic license in our quest to help kids make some sense of it all without going too far down the rabbit hole of linguistics.

The learning curve might seem a bit steep to some, but we ask you to try it and see. We were surprised at our students' progress.

Our textbooks are available in two forms:
1. Regular mainstream phonics
2. Specifically for Korean ESL students.

Our website is www.supercrazyfun.net.

And this is the whole team:

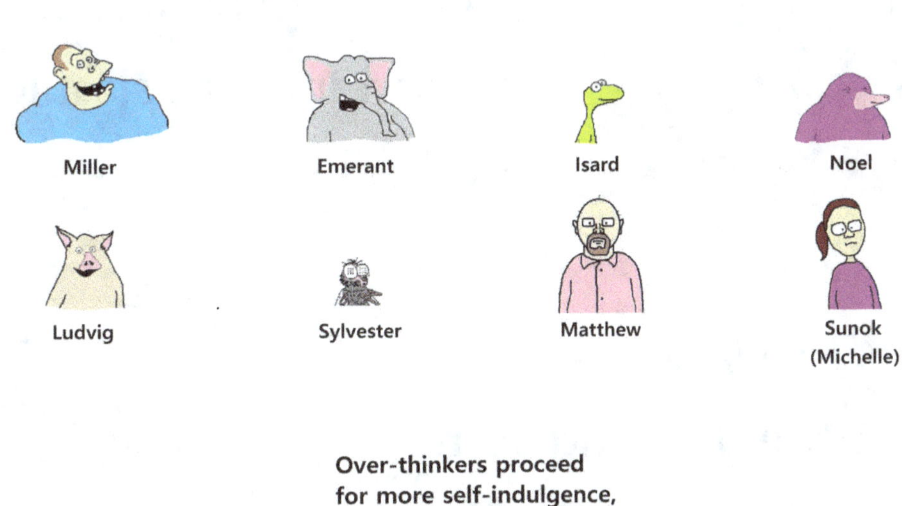

If you thought THAT was boring, try reading this:

The colored letters in this book do actually have a function, right from the start.

a b c d e f g h i j k l m n o p

To many of the kids reading this, the colors are just something pleasing to the eye intended to make the experience a little more interesting.

And to many others they are clearly highlighting something important that should be noticed.

But some actually notice a pattern that brings along some extra information about sounds.

The colors are related to the **qualities** of the sounds.

Vowels are two different colors because some are shorter and more aggressive in their sound.

Some consonants are able to go on and on until breath is exhausted, and some are quite short and sharp. Also, some have a voice, and some do not.

So... red denotes a sound that is not voiced, and blue denotes one that is voiced. A lighter shade denotes a sound that can go on and on, and a darker shade denotes one that cannot. Q is purple because it is both voiced and not voiced, and magic E is grey. This pattern is in chapters 1 to 3. The final chapters employ different strategies. At the very least, it's colorful.

Contents

Chapter 1

THE ALPHABET

Welcome!

Hello. I am a gorilla that wants to be a super hero. My super power is making the alphabet sounds!

Can you make them too?

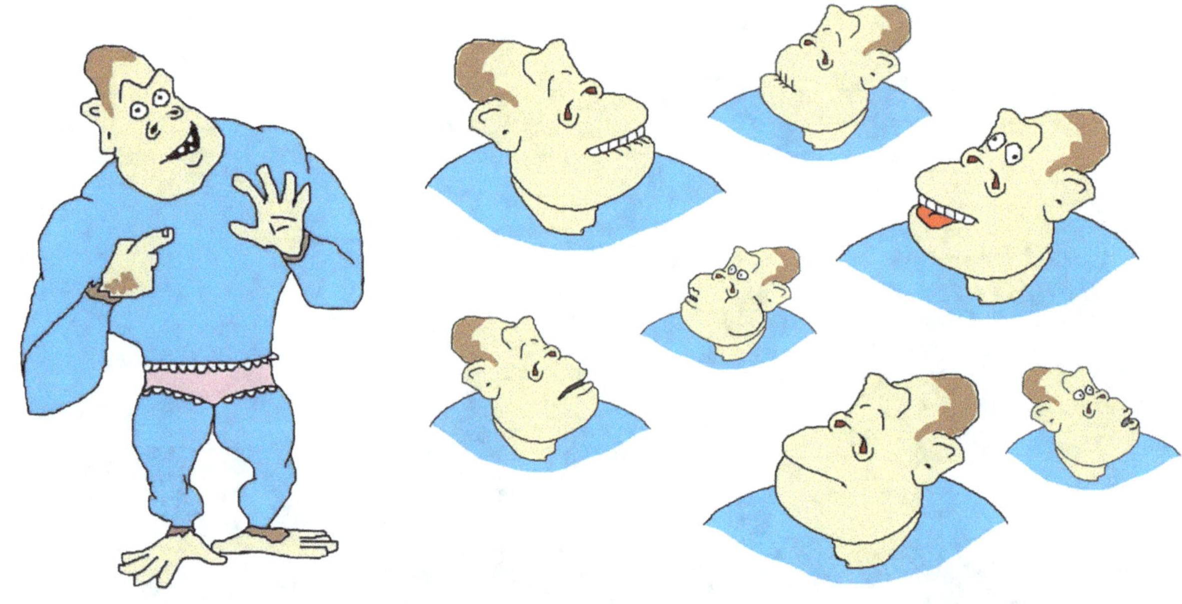

And I'm an elephant. I'm quite wide.

Have you noticed some alphabet letters are wide?

Hello. I'm a mole.
I like to dig.

Some letters like to dig too.
Can you guess which ones?

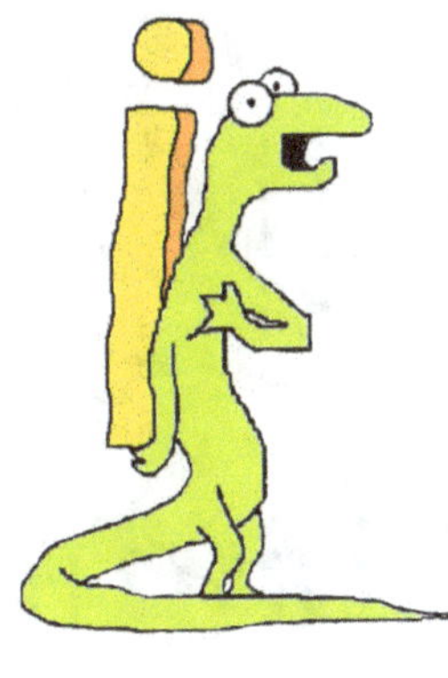

I'm a lizard. I'm quite thin.

Have you noticed
some letters are also thin?

And I'm smelly.

We are going to
show you all about
reading!

A

apple

angry

B

banana

bird

C

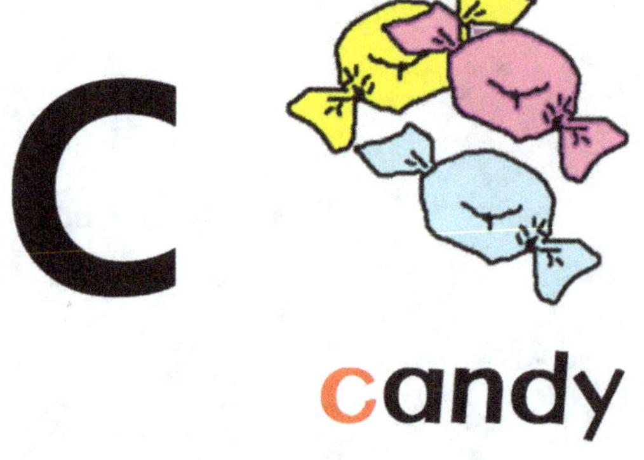

candy

cat

cup

An apple and a banana
An apple and a banana
An apple and a banana
And an angry cat

A cup and candy
A cup and candy
A cup and candy
And an angry bird

A

alligator

ant

B

baby

book

C

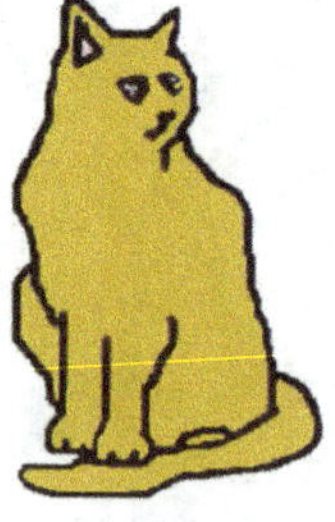

cat

WAA!
An angry baby.

WAA!
An angry cat.

WAA!
An angry alligator.

An angry banana?!

D

desk

diamond

E

elbow

elephant

F

fish

frog

A fish and a frog
and an elephant elbow
All on a diamond desk

A book and a cup
and an angry ant
All on a diamond desk

D

dog

E

egg

F

flower

A dog.

Flowers.

A dog in the flowers.

A dog egg in the flowers.

G 

gold

good

H 

hat

house

I 

ill

in

Ill in a hat
Ill in a good hat
Ill in a good gold hat

Ill in a house
Ill in a good house
Ill in a good gold house

G

gorilla

grass

H

hill

I

insect

Grass on a hill.

A happy insect in the grass
on a hill.

A happy gorilla on a hill.

No happy insect in the grass
on a hill.

J

jam

K

kangaroo

L

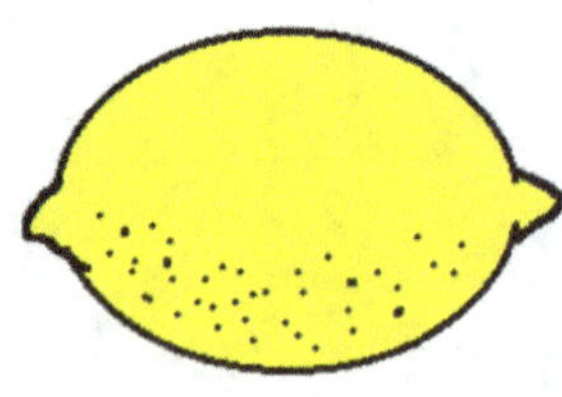 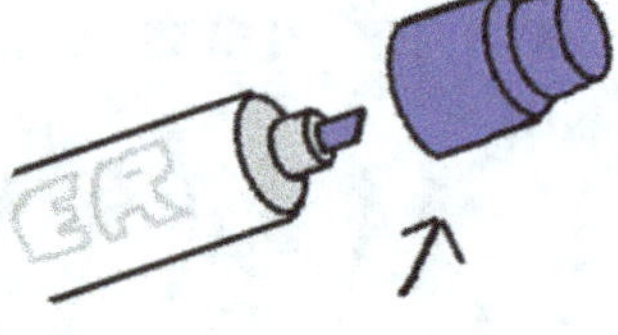 

lemon   **l**id   **l**ion

Lemon jam
Lemon jam
Lift the lid
Kangaroos like lemon jam

Kangaroo jam
Kangaroo jam
Lift the lid
Lions like kangaroo jam

J

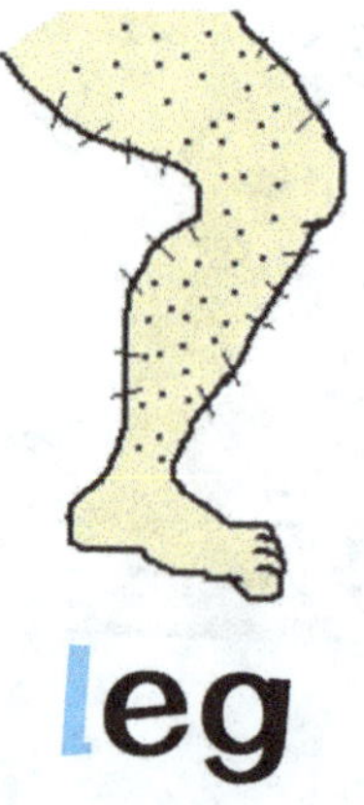

jail

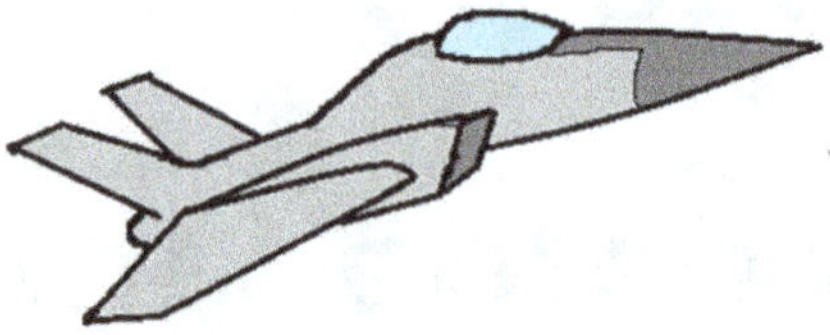

jet

jump

K

key

kick

L

leg

Lion and kangaroo in jail.

Kick the leg!
Get the key!

Jump in the jet!

Lion in jail.

Did you know, letters sometimes have different sounds?

Sometimes we say a letter's NAME instead of its usual sound.

It's mostly just these letters though:

 apple

 acorn

 egg

 eagle

 igloo

 ice cream

 on

 old

 up

 unicorn

M

milk

monkey

N

no

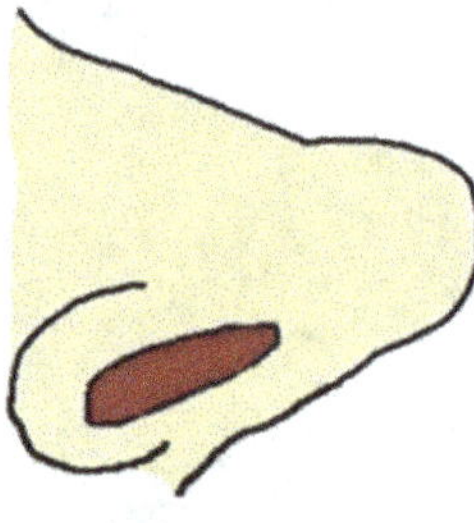

nose

O

octopus

old

Old monkey milk
and an octopus nose
Old monkey milk
and an octopus nose
On no!
Old monkey milk!

M

moon

mouse

N

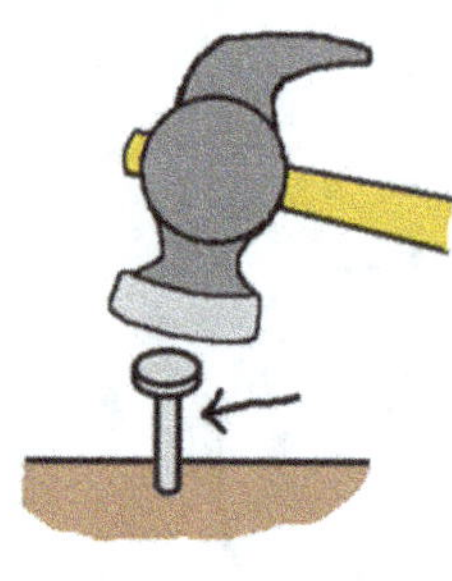

nail

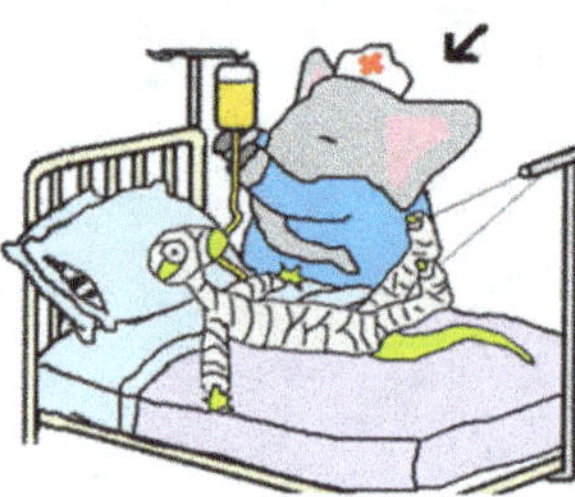

nurse

O

ox

ostrich

Ox and mouse and ostrich
on the moon.

A nail! Get the nail!

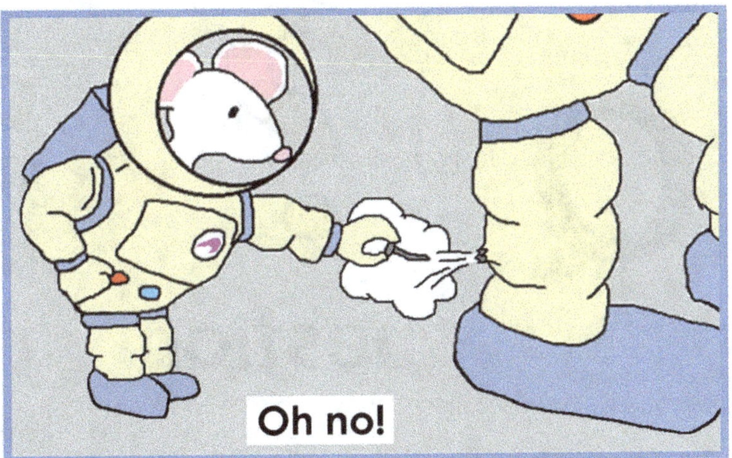

Ox and mouse and ostrich
and a nurse.

P

pants

poop

Q

question

quick

quiet

R

really

A quick quiet question:
Did you poop your pants?
A quick quiet question:
Did you poop your pants?
Yes I did!
I really did!
I did poop my pants!

P

peach

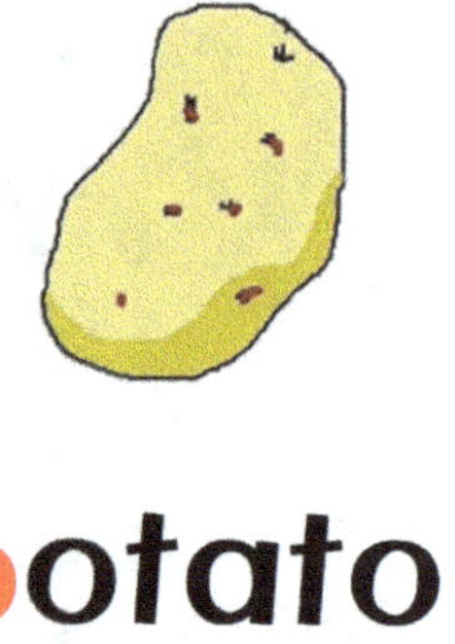

potato

Q

queen

R

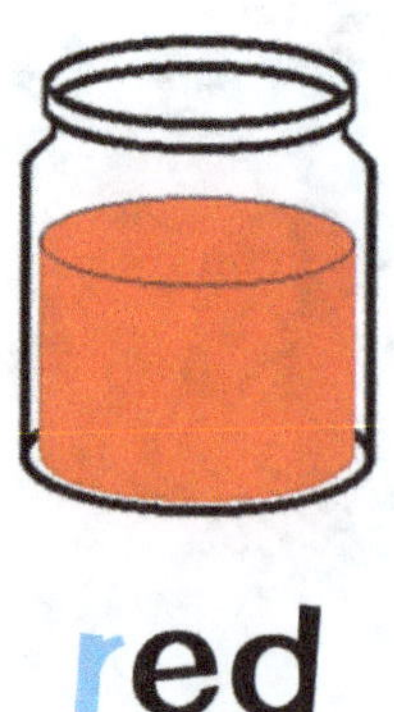

red

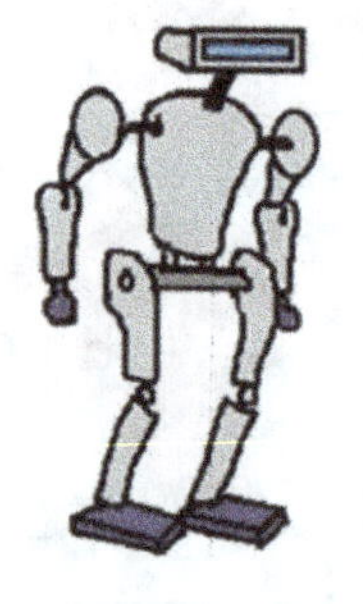

robot

run

The Queen's Red Robot
The Queen's
Peach & Potato
House

The queen has a red robot.

My red robot puts a peach and a potato..

Run, red robot! Run!
Really!!

S

sad

sit

sun

T

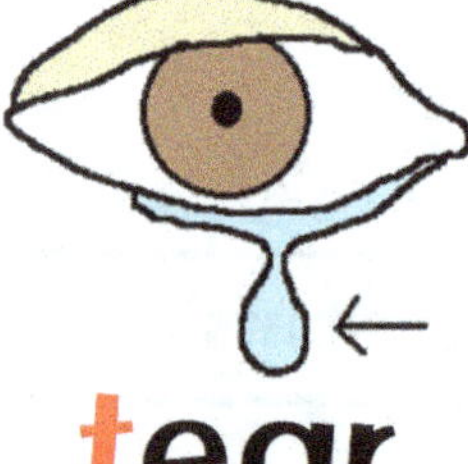

tear

tiger

U

umbrella

under

V

violin

Sad tiger sits
Under the sun
Tiger tears
Tiger tears
One by one

Sad tiger sits
Under an umbrella
Violins! Violins!
Sad cage dweller

S

smell

time

T

umpire

U

V

van

vest

vomit

The umpire says, "Time!"

Go to the van.
Get a red vest.

The red vest smells.

The red team wins!
vomit!
vomit!

W

wish

X

box

box

fox

Y

Z

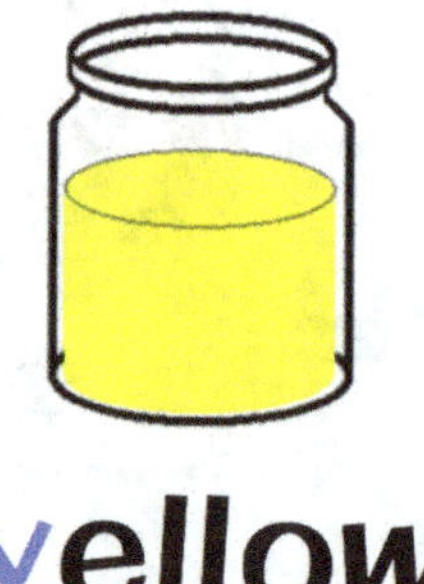

yellow

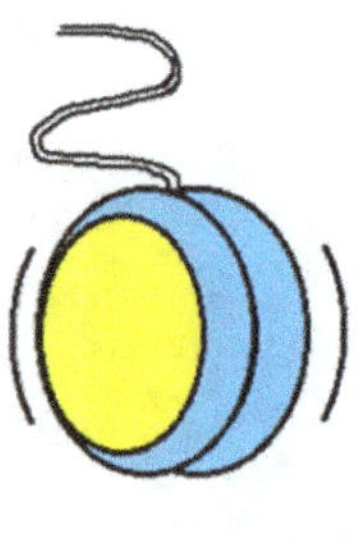

yo yo

zebra

I wish I had a zebra
I wish I had a fox
I wish I had a yo yo
All in a yellow box
I wish I did
I wish I did
I wish it had a yellow lid!

W

wait

water

wave

X

fix

Y

yawn

yikes

young

Z

zero

zipper

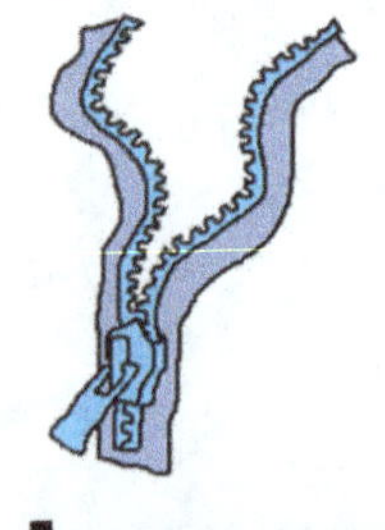

Six young zebras
wait in the water.

A wave! Quick! Fix the zipper!

Yikes!

Zero young zebras
wait in the water.
YAWN~

Have you noticed that sometimes A makes the U sound?

And sometimes U and O
both make the same sound:

Of course, it's not just
A, E, I, O and U that have
"sometimes sounds."

When X is the first letter of
a word, it uses another
letter's sound!

It's very strange, isn't it?

Chapter 2

SHORT WORDS

Welcome to short words!

Hello. Did you know we make words by putting letters together?

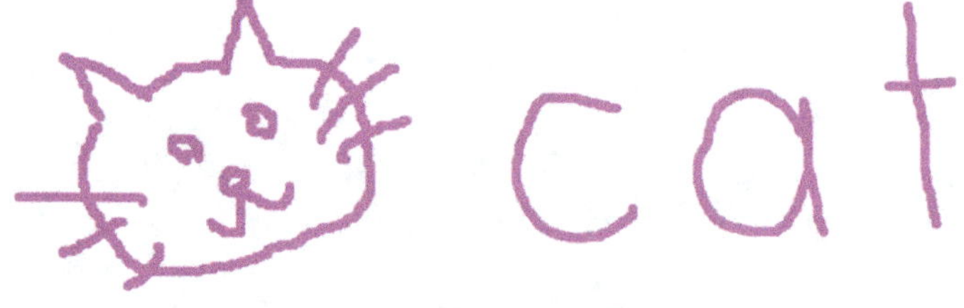

We just put them side by side!

Then we do our best to make the right matching sounds!

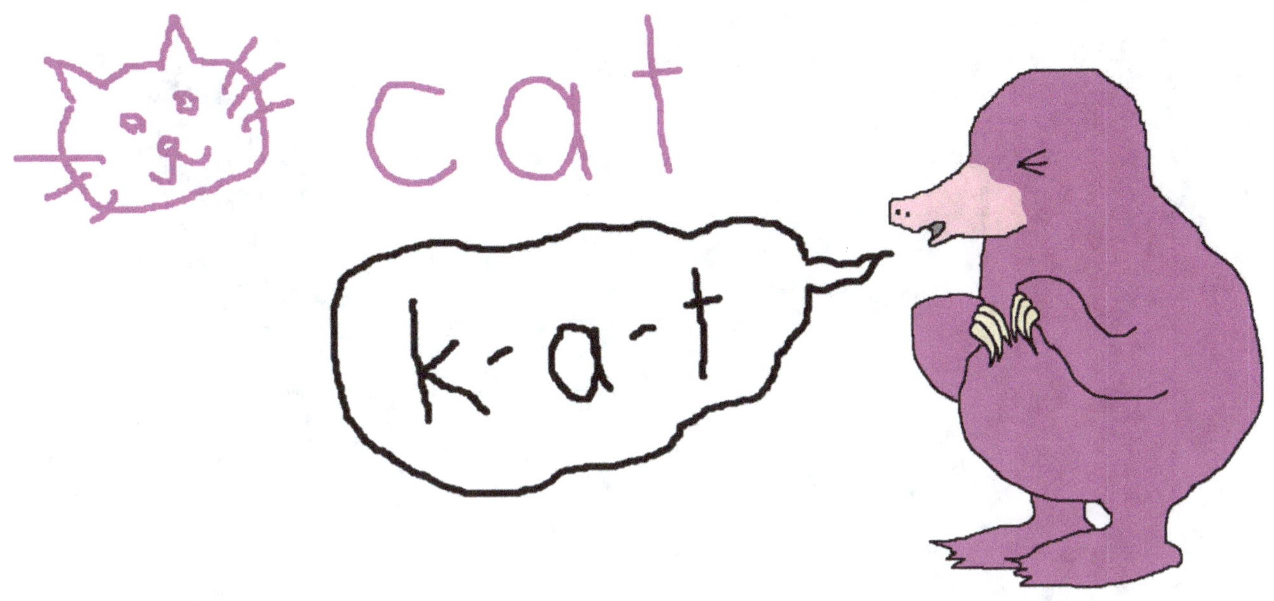

Finally we smoothly join them into one sound.

bad

fan

man

nag

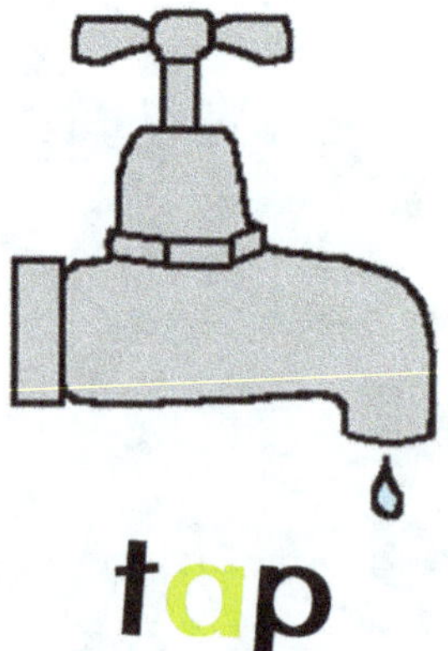

tap

Nag the man
Nag the man
Nag the bad man

"Turn off the tap!"
"Turn off the fan!"

Nag the man
Nag the man
Nag the bad man

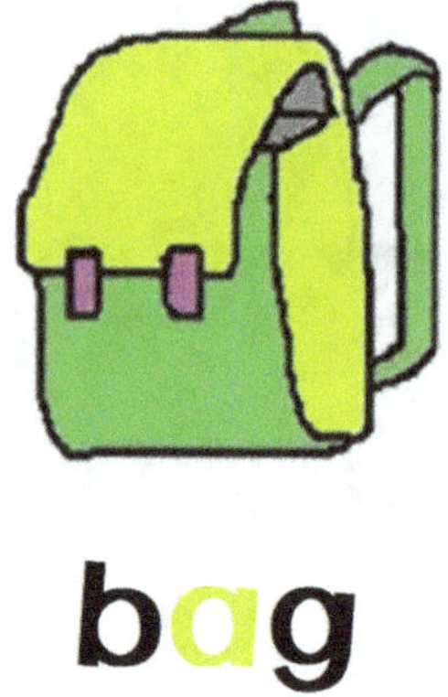

bag

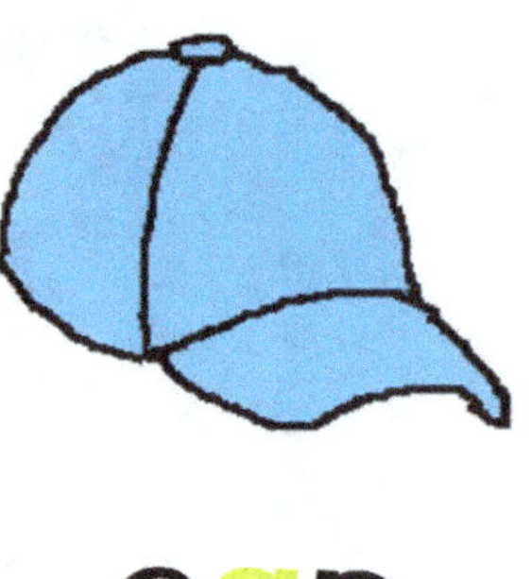

cap

ham

jam

fat

rat

In my bag I have a cap

...and that.

It is yummy.

It has ham...and jam

...and...what is that?

A fat rat!

Deb

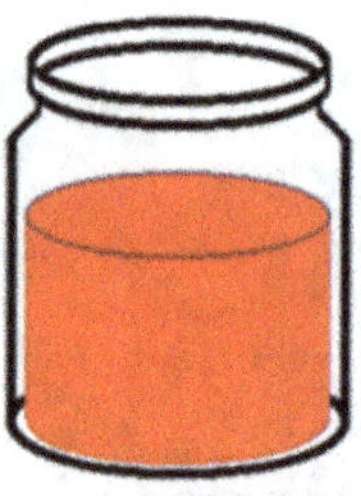

red

wed

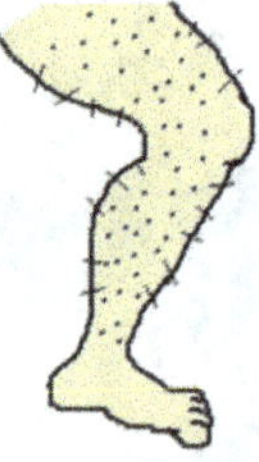

leg

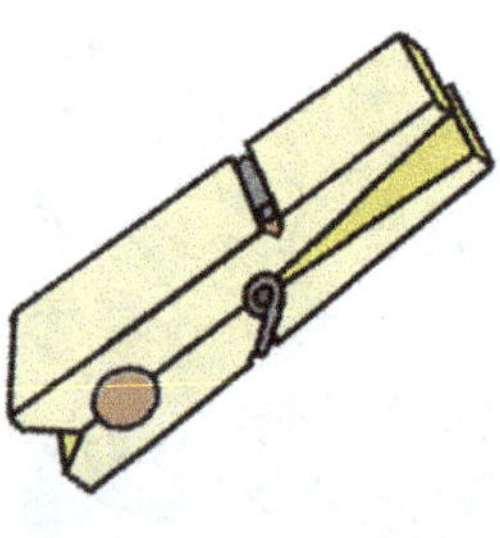

peg

Peg leg Deb
She wears red
She's so scary
Peg leg Deb

Peg leg Deb
I will wed
She's not scary
Peg leg Deb

men

net

pet

wet

web

well

You men!
My pet is in the well!

I will get your pet with a net.

Scary webs ...and I am wet!

Sorry. No pet in my net.

MY PET!!

Oh my pet.
Was it wet in that well?

bib

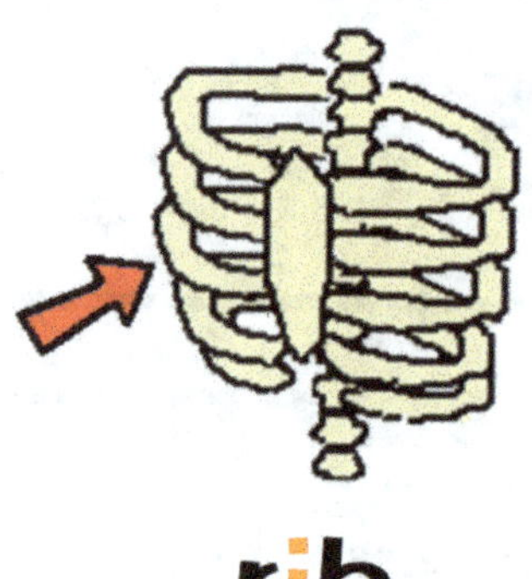

rib

big

kid

sit

Big kid sits
in a bib
Big kid sits
in a bib

"I want ribs!"
"Give me ribs!"

Big kid sits
in a bib

bi**n**

fi**n**

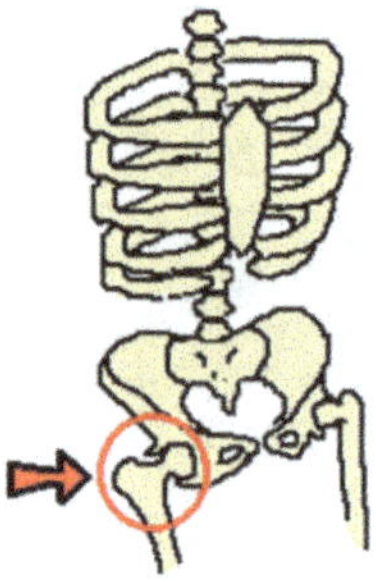

hip

ri**p**

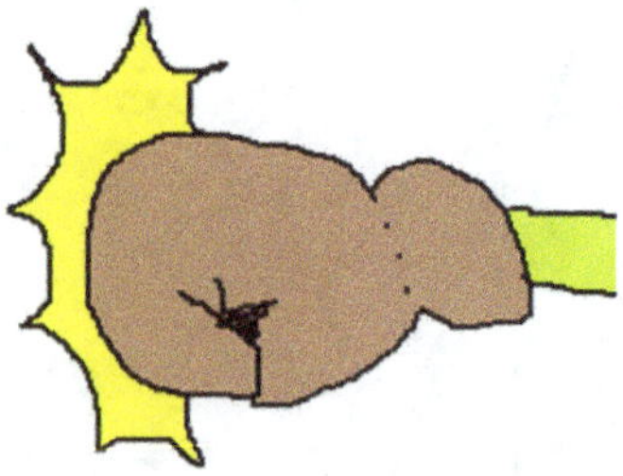

hit

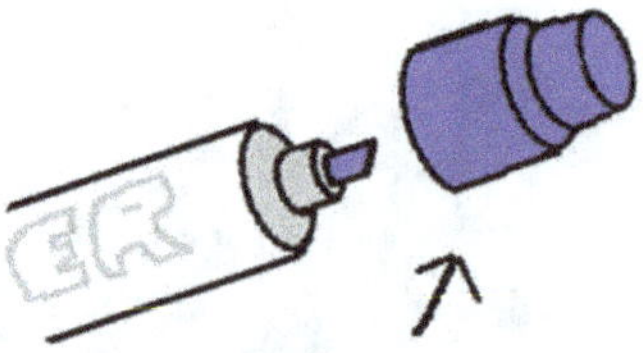

li**d**

*w*i*g*

I am Fin Man!

I have a big fin!
rip!

And fins on my hips!

And I wear a wig...
hit!

I am Fin Man!

Put him in the bin
and shut the lid.

The Story of Soft H

**Did you know?
H is the softest
of all letters,
but soft doesn't
mean weak!**

**H has the power
to soften other
letters!**

th sounds like this: 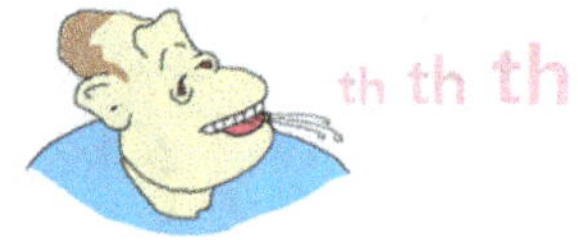

sh sounds like this: 

ch sounds like this: 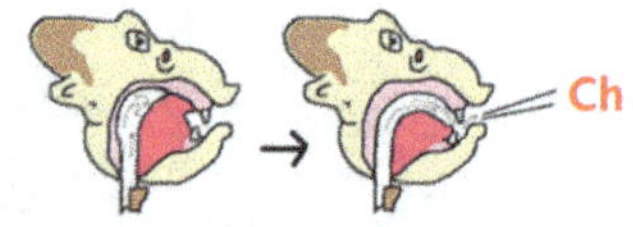

ph sounds like this: 

wh **sometimes sounds softer too!**

The Story of Soft H

Long ago, T,P,C,S, and W all softened their sound next to H. Only W stopped doing this.

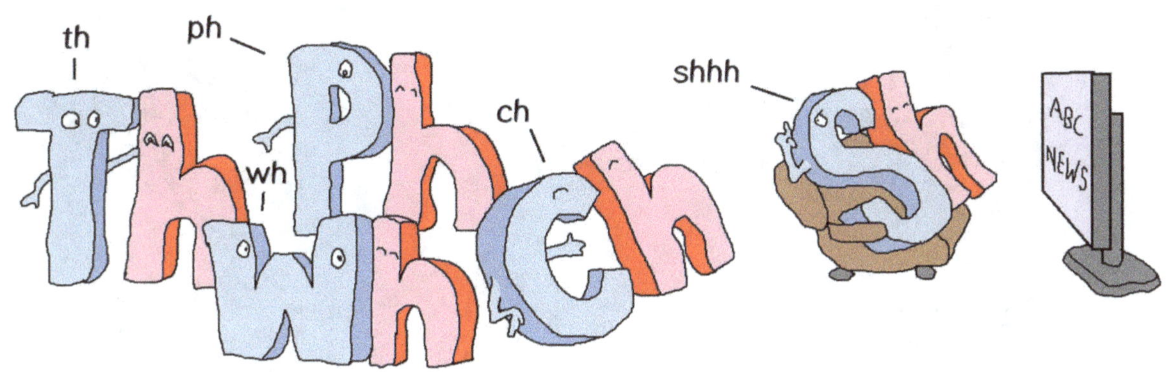

W was very polite.
W even let H go first!

But then with time
W got bigger.

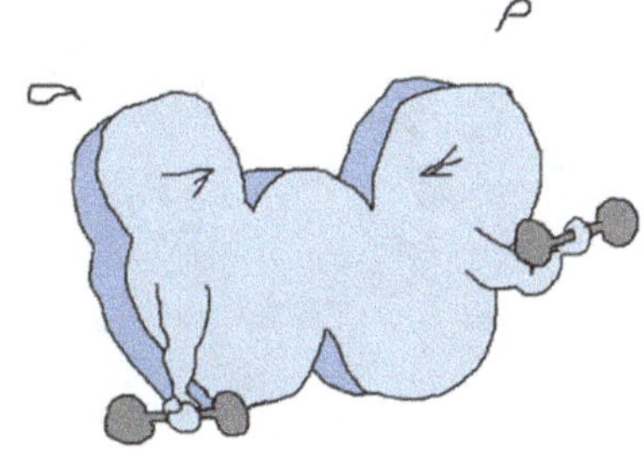

W soon forgot H was even there!

Strangely though, W is quiet when they meet O.

dog

log

on

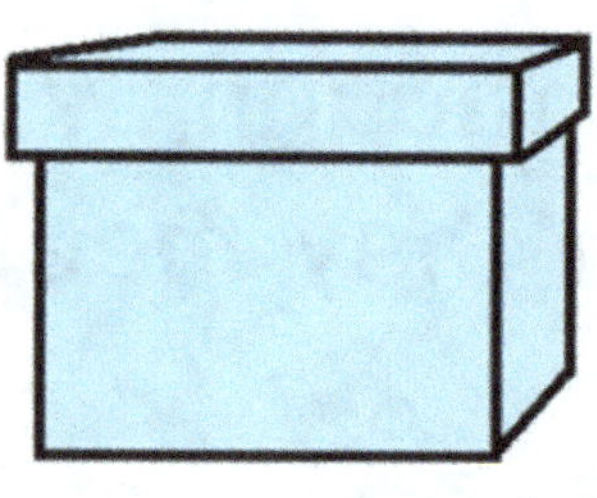

box

fox

Dog on a log
Dog on a log
He's a handsome
Dog on a log

Fox in a box
Fox in a box
She's a pretty
Fox in a box

rob

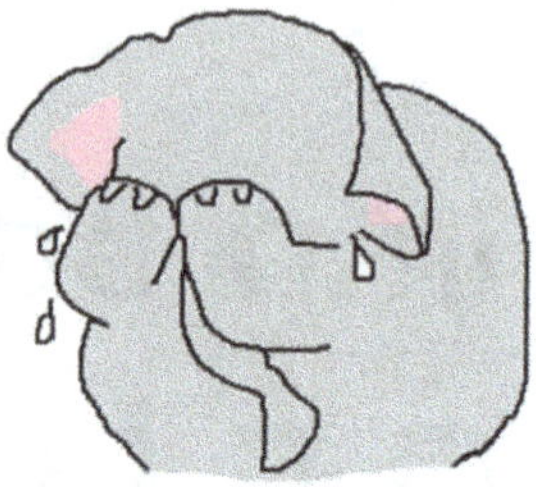

sob

Ron

hop

mop

shop

got

not

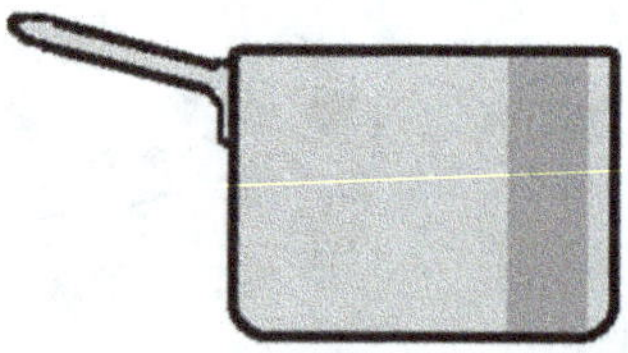

pot

Let's rob Ron's shop!
RON'S SHOP
LOTS OF POTS AND MOPS
RON

I talk... you rob the shop.

Hi Ron!
Hello!
hop
RON

Do you want a mop or pot?
No. I do not.
hop
ROB

I got a mop and a pot...
RON'S SHOP
LOTS OF POTS AND MOPS
?

...and ten cents!!
Sob, sob.

fun

run

jump

mud

pup

tub

Run pup
Run pup, run
Run in the mud
It's fun fun fun!

Run pup
Run pup, run
Jump in the tub
It's fun fun fun!

b**u****g**

h**u****g**

c**u****t**

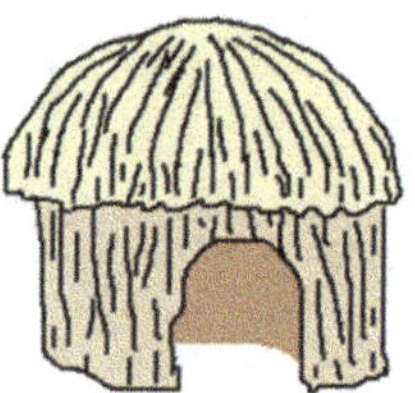

h**u****t**

b**u****d**

c**u****p**

s**u****b**

Stop the sub!   I see buds!

Wait! I see huts!
No! We want buds!

Cut the buds.
Put them in cups.

Bugs!
Run to the sub!

Ha ha! We want your sub!

Have fun with the bugs!
hug~

bus

cop

get

hot

pig

Hot pig on the bus
Get a net!

Hot pig on the bus
Get a net!

Call a cop!

Call a cop!

Get a net!

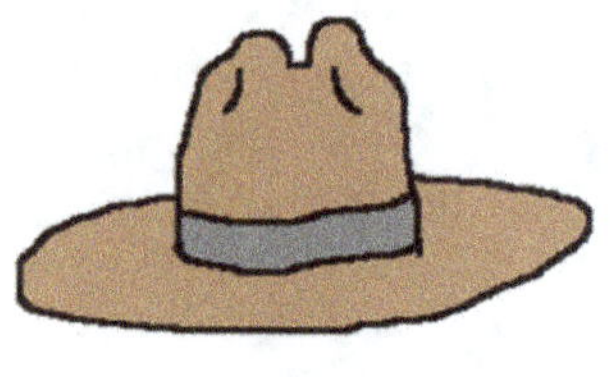

hat

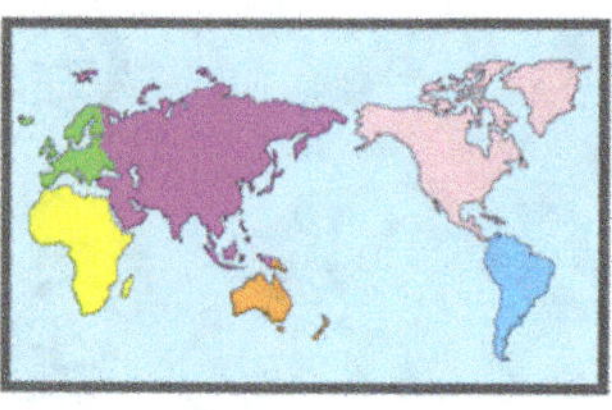

map

pan

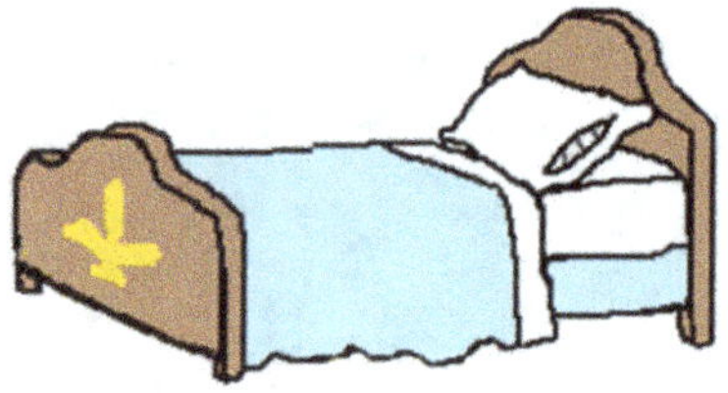

bed

win

jug

You must go on the bus.

You will need a hat.
And a map.

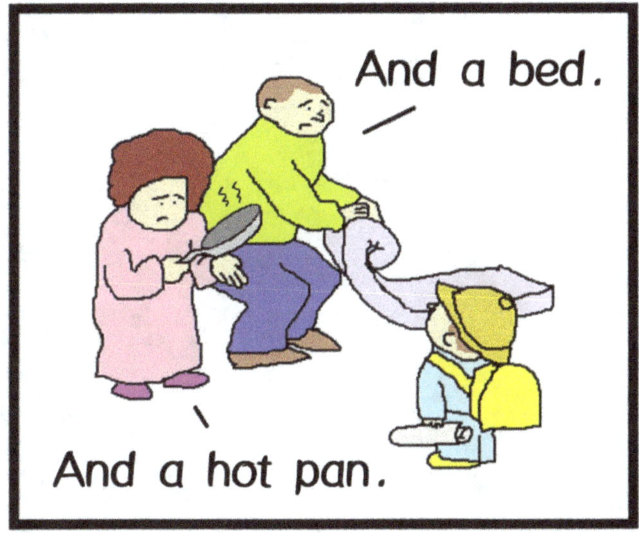

And a bed.
And a hot pan.

And a jug! And a net!

Go, and win, win, win!

Hop on, kids!
KINDERGARTEN BUS

Chapter 3

LONG VOWELS

Welcome to long vowels!

Did you know?
Letters sometimes have strange rules.

There is a letter that is allowed to use magic!

We call it Magic E, and it is silent...
Like a ninja!

It uses its magic to make its friends say their NAMES instead of their sounds!

But it can't just do it willy-nilly!
In this book, it must be last in line!

The vowel's name is also the long vowel!

But these days we think that rule is a bit unfair to E's friends, so instead we ask the Split Digraphs to help make the long vowel!

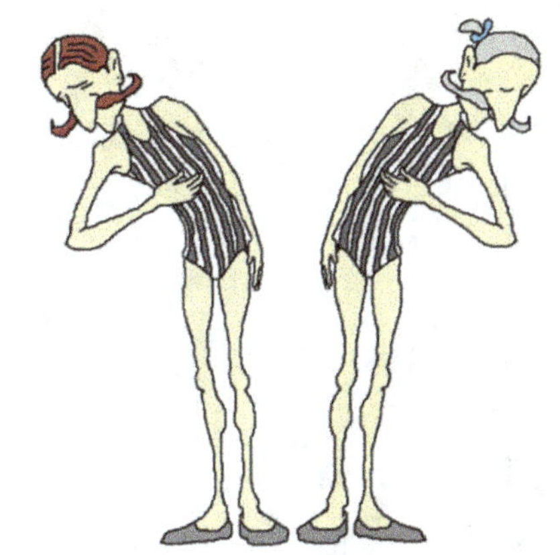

Still, some people suspect Magic E is often up to his old tricks!

Ask your teacher.

a_e

ape

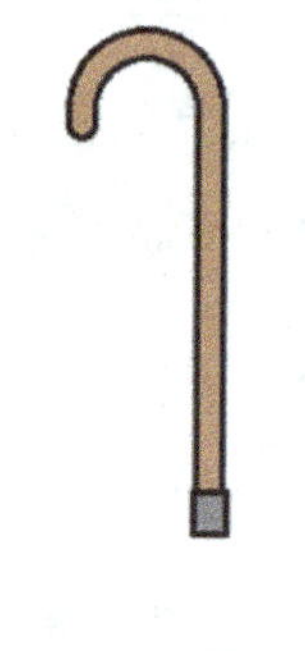

cane

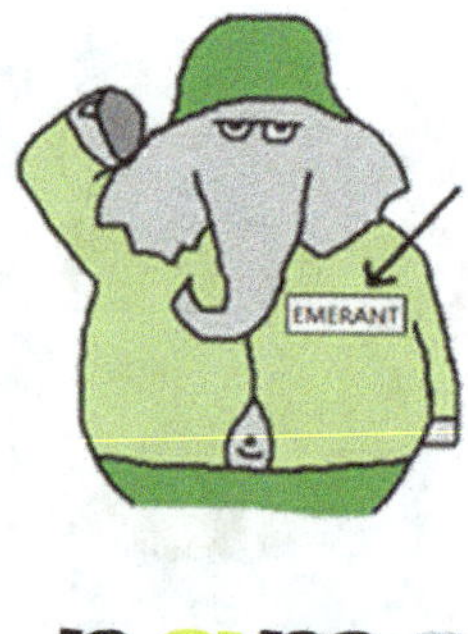

name

cape

hate

same

That ape has the same name!
That ape has the same cane!
That ape has the same cape!

I hate that
same name
same cane
same cape
ape!

bake    **cake**    **lake**    **rake**

game 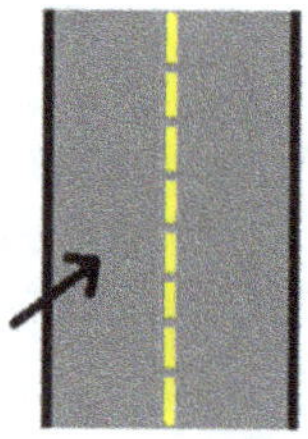   **lane**    **mane** 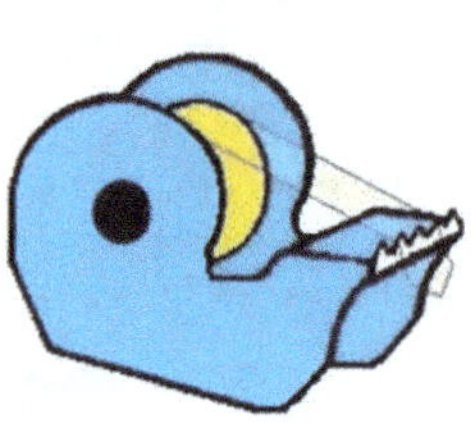   **tape**

gate    **late** 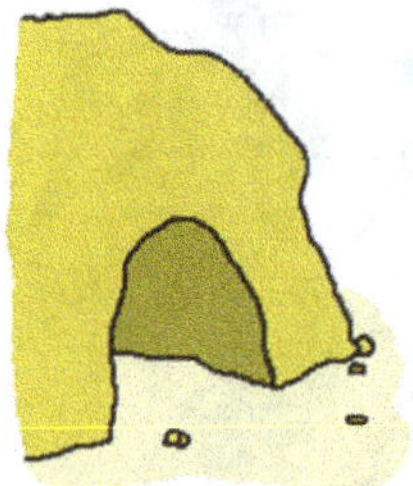   **cave**    **save**

Don't play that game!
Take us to the lake!

But first, brush your mane.

And rake the cave.

I will bake a cake to take.

And you fix the gate.

Fix it with tape.

Save time. Take that lane.

Not this lane... that lane!

We are too late!

"SOMETIMES SOUNDS"

Did you know?

C's "sometimes sound" is s!

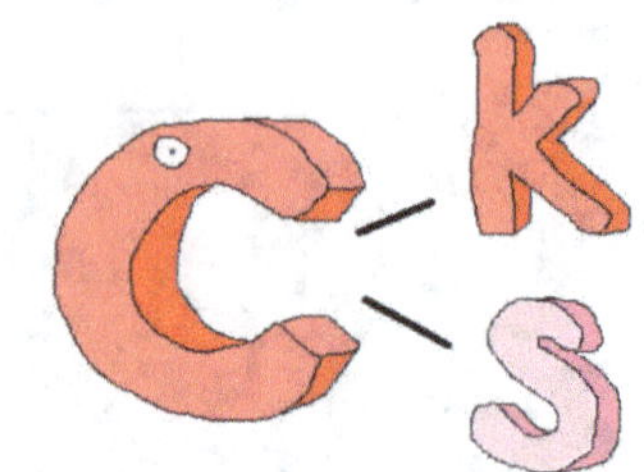

And G's "sometimes sound" is j!

E's magic changes them, too!

S often changes as well,
but Z doesn't like it!

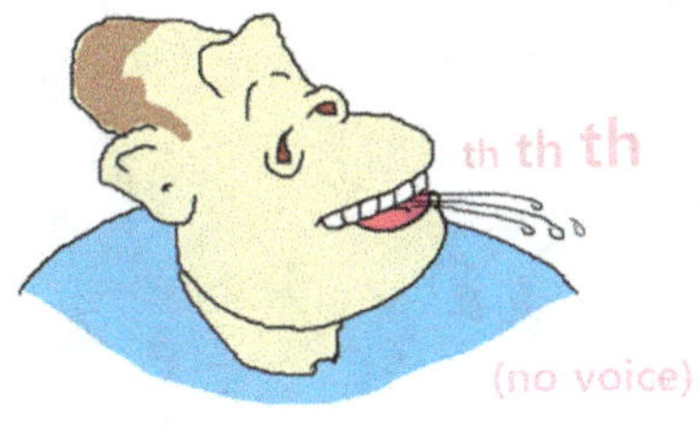

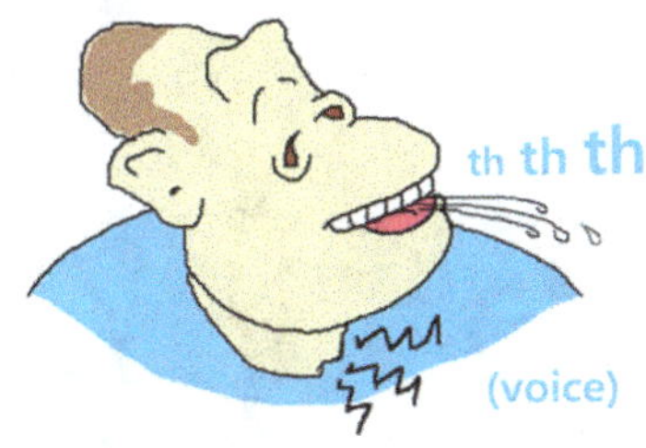

Perhaps you have already noticed that "th" also has two sounds.

E's magic changes that, too!

Sometimes U cuts the "y" sound off the start of its name when E's magic strikes!

But one letter doesn't change: O is so impressed with R...

...that it ignores E when they're together!

Ev**e**

St**e**v**e**

m**e**m**e**

th**e**m**e**

sc**e**n**e**

Chin**es**e

Japan**es**e

extr**e**m**e**

Eve's meme has a
Chinese theme

Steve's meme has a
Japanese theme

Whose meme will
make the scene?

The meme theme scene
is so extreme!

her**e**

mer**e**

Pet**e**

dele**t**e

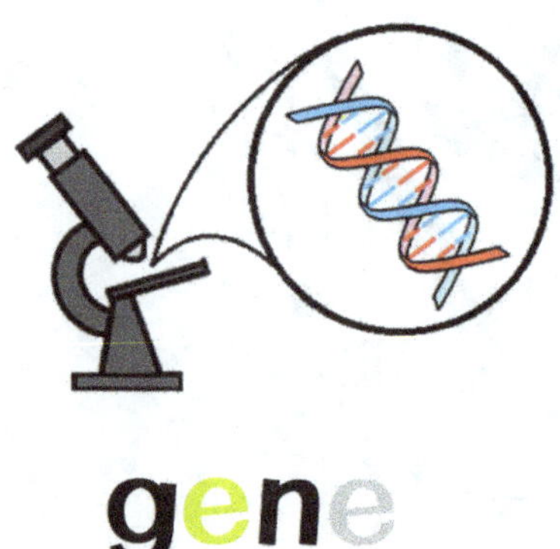

gen**e**

supre**m**e

Our team has a new theme!

The theme is "Delete One Gene."

Delete one gene
and we can be the BEST TEAM!

I can delete one gene here and now!

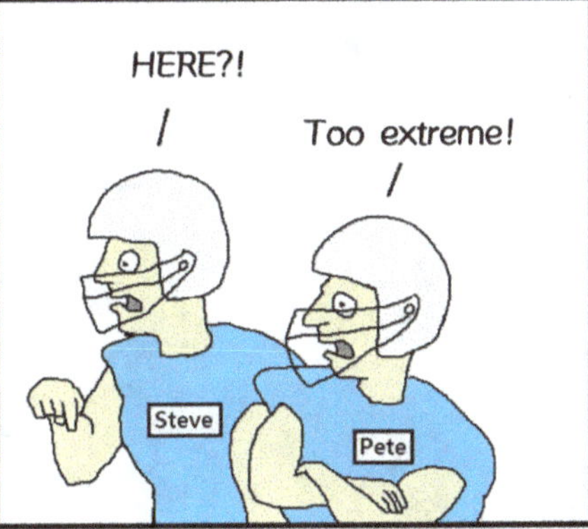
HERE?!
Too extreme!
Steve
Pete

Pete and I will leave the team!

Pete! Steve! See the scene.
Pete
Steve

Delete one MERE gene
and you can be SUPREME!

BEST TEAM 2021

bike

hike

like

five

hive

kite

nine

ride

I like to hike and ride a bike
Nine to five I'm at the hive

But after five I like to hike

I like to hike and ride a bike
And maybe even fly a kite!

hide

wide

Ike

Mike

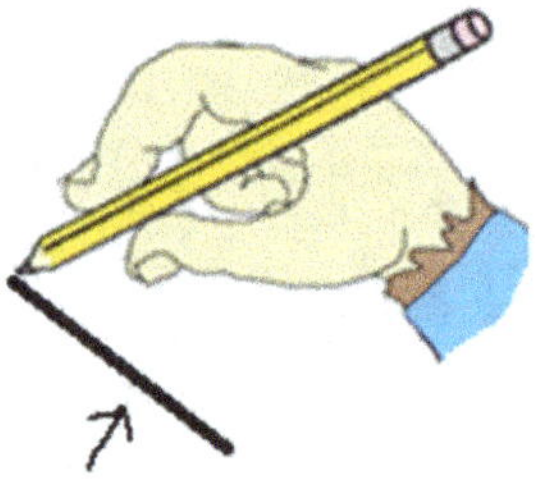

line

mine

pipe

ripe

wipe

bite

site

dive

Ike, Mike, hike to the site and wipe the wide pipe.

Next, ride the line to the mine and hide.

Next, find nine ripe bananas and bite five.

Now, ride a bike to the lake
AND DIVE IN!

Hello Ike?
Hello Mike?

Ike?
Mike?

o_e

ho**l**e

mo**l**e

ho**p**e

no**t**e

vo**t**e

Vote for Mole!
Vote for Mole!
He's the best mole in the hole

All your hopes
He's taking notes

Vote for Mole!
Vote for Mole!
He's the best mole in the hole!

joke poke yoke home

bone cone zone

lobe robe mope rope

Hello kids.
Put on your hat and robe.

Go to your Home Room Zone.
HOME
ROOM
ZONE
EVE
PETE

Eve, go to Cone Zone.
cone
EVE
PETE

Pete, go to Rope Zone.
rope
EVE
PETE

Rope Zone!
Cone Zone!

I hope you like your zone.
HOME
ROOM
ZONE

Cone Zone has games and jokes.

Rope Zone has no games or jokes.
...and you must wear a yoke.

But do not mope!
We also poke your nose and lobes
with BONES!

u_e

cute

lute

mule

ruse

tune

Cute mule plays a tune
On its lute

Cute mule plays a tune
On its lute

It's a ruse!
It's a ruse!

A mule can't play the lute!

cub**e** jub**e** tub**e** us**e**

rul**e** Yul**e** dun**e** Jun**e**

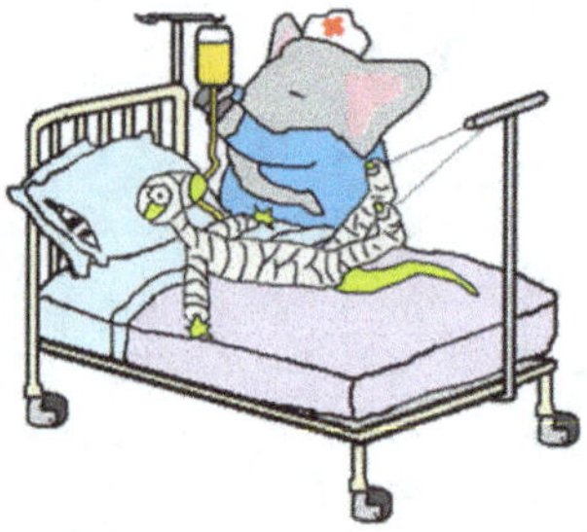

cur**e** lur**e** pur**e** mut**e**

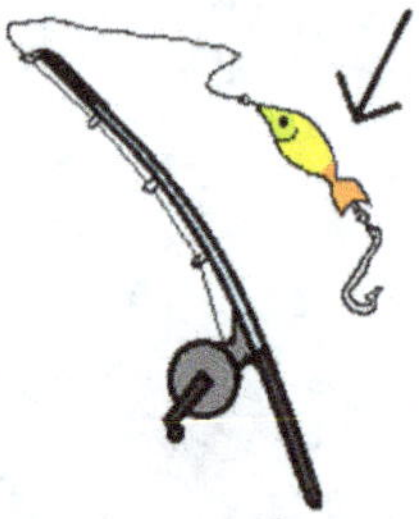

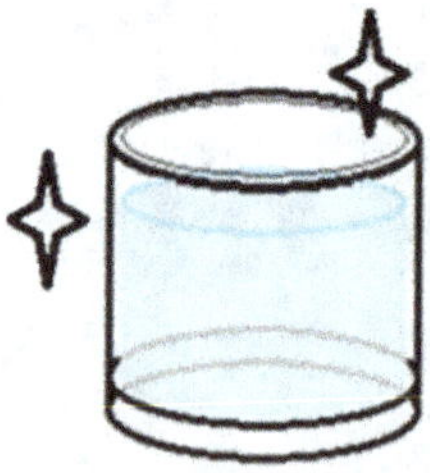

THE DOCTOR IN THE DUNE
Hello Doctor.
Hello. Happy Yule!

He ate a jube and now... he is mute.
.....

He ate the jube in June.
In JUNE?! It is Yule now!

What is the cure?
A lure!

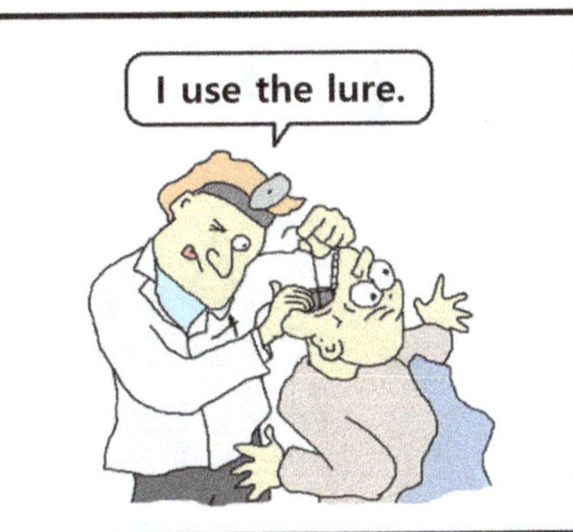

I use the lure.

I got the jube!
.....
But he is still mute!

Hmm... the best cure is... POOP!
....?

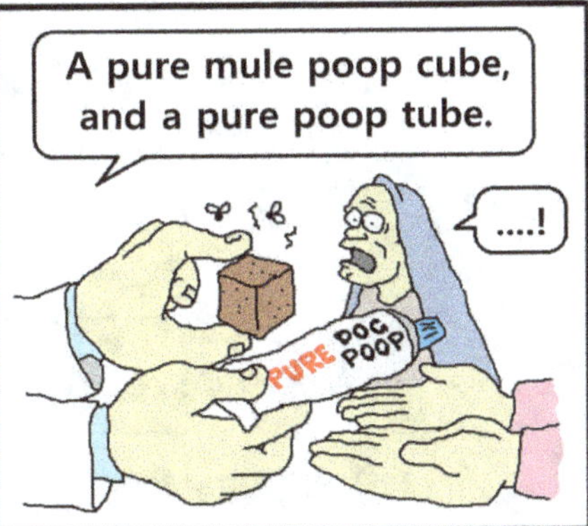

A pure mule poop cube, and a pure poop tube.
....!
PURE DOC POOP

Make pure mule poop soup.
That is my rule.
....!

duke

Luke

uke

more

sore

fire

wire

made

Duke Luke played his uke
It made his fingers sore

The uke wire
Lit on fire

And the people yelled
"More! More!"

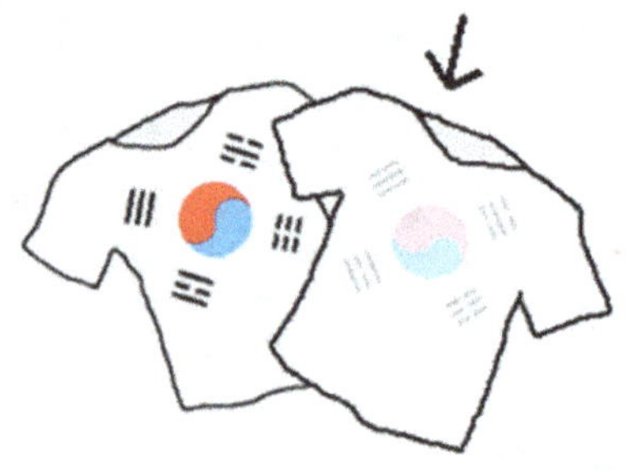

fa**d**e

wa**d**e

e**k**e

pe**k**e

ni**c**e

ti**r**e

bo**r**e

hu**g**e

My Love...
I made a poem
...for you

I will wade into a lake...

And I will bake a birthday cake...
...for you

I will rope the dragon's fire...

And I will fix your bike tire...
...for you

I will eke and eke and eke...

And I will even walk your peke...
...for you

For you, nice maid...
My love will never fade.

You are a huge bore.

The Rebellious Words

Sometimes when Magic E is asleep
and the Split Digraphs are busy...

...the words that don't like to follow rules come out to play.

Some words just have to give us trouble. They love to break the rules!

Chapter 4

CONSONANT BLENDS

(and a few other consonant digraphs snuck in)

Welcome to consonant blends!

Hello. Did you know?

Some letters are a bit more difficult to put together smoothly.

We have to "blend" them!

But we don't actually put them in a blender.

It's more like we just let them go down the water slide together!

"Blends" have to sit
very close together to
make the sound we
want.

I'm not sure they are
very comfortable.

So let's look at how letters blend, but not
the letters we call "vowels," A,E,I,O, and U.

Some of them can "blend" too, but let's
just look at all the other letters this time.

The Story of Y...the Spy!

A, E, I, O, and U are called "vowels," and the rest of the letters are called "consonants."

They are two separate groups, but one of the consonants works with the vowels!

Y is a consonant, but it wants to be a vowel.

Y can work as I, and the long E sound too!

And...

The Story of Wh

When W stopped softening its sound around H, they didn't really like being in that group anymore.

Also, they were the only pair that couldn't end a word.

It's not surprising they made different friends.

Can you guess what their new friends all have in common?

black

flag

cliff

crash

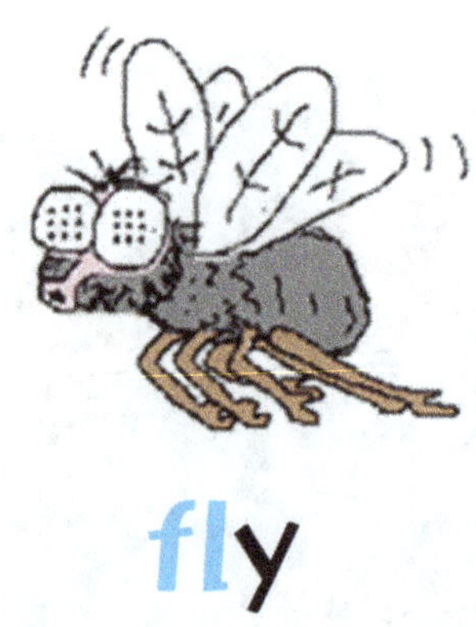

fly

fry

Fly the flag
Fly the flag
Fly the black flag!

Crash into a cliff

Fry the flag
Fry the flag
Fry the black flag!

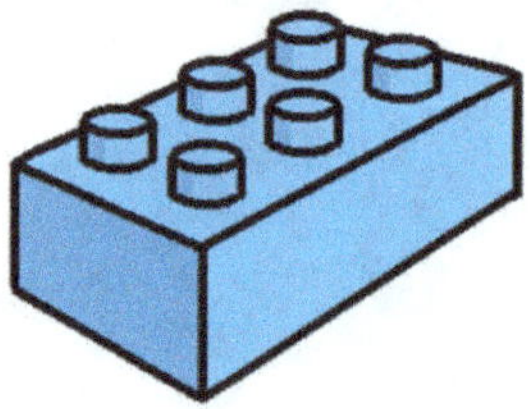

block

brag

brick

clock

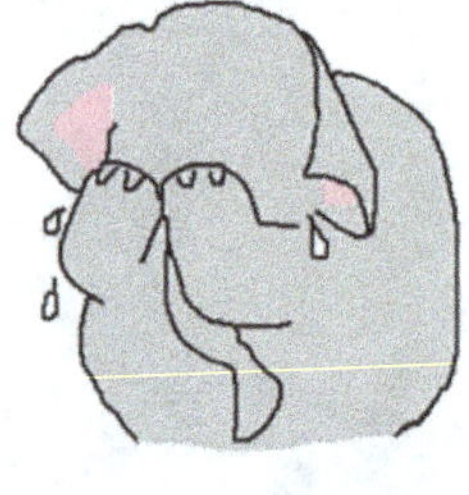

cry

free

In Jail

Look!
!

Blocks! Not bricks!

We can make a T- Rex!

NO! We can make a hole!

We can be FREE!

I'll go first. Your turn at 4 o'clock.
Okay.

At 4 o'clock:

Everyone! Come see my T-Rex!

Look! I made it from blocks!

Brag, brag...

Don't cry...
You can play with T-Rex.

sl gl gr pl pr dr

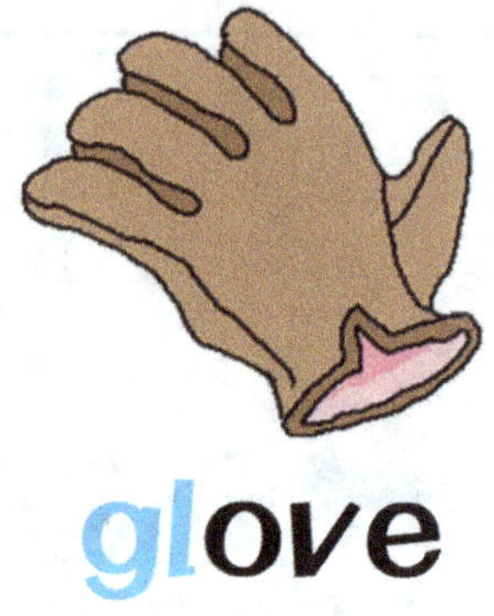

glove

green

dress

press

price

Green dress and gloves!
Green dress and gloves!
Press your face onto the glass
Green dress and gloves!

Green dress and gloves!
Green dress and gloves!
What's the price?
What's the price?
Green dress and gloves!

drive

plan

plum

grape

sled

slide

slime

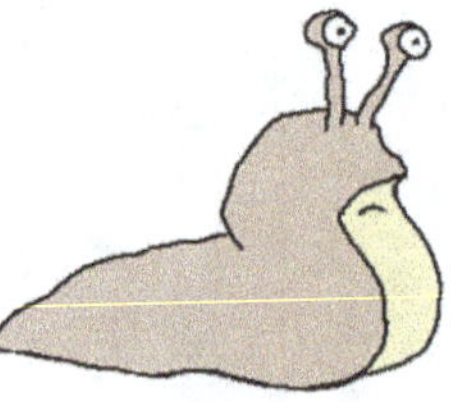

slug

The Ants' Plan

Sir! We can move grapes.

But plums are too big!

I have a plan, Sir.

First, we make some sleds.

Next, we get some slugs.

Slugs make slime...

...and sleds slide on slime.

We drive the sleds!   Good plan!

(LATER)
Ready... DRIVE!

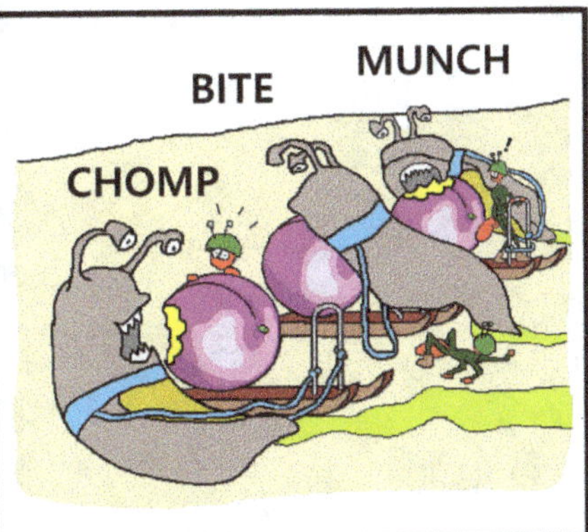
BITE
MUNCH
CHOMP

I have another plan, Sir...
z z z

cold

wild

hunt

plant

tank

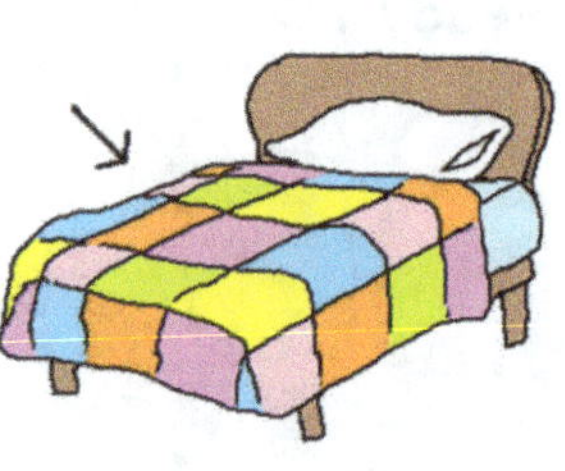

quilt

Hunt, hunt the wild wild plant
Put it in the zoo

A tank for the hunt
A quilt for the cold
A hat and gloves too

Hunt, hunt the wild wild plant
Maybe I need glue...

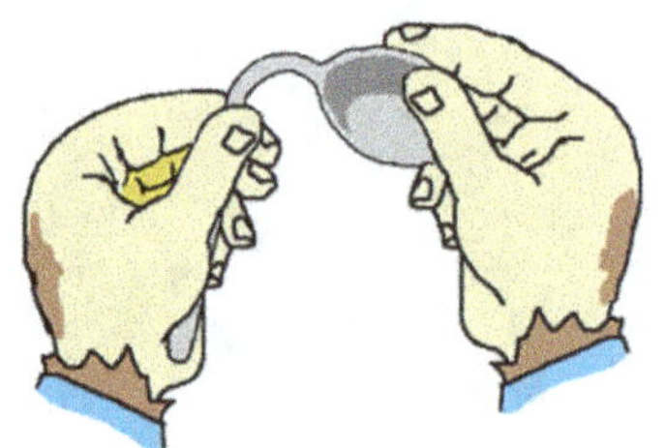

bend

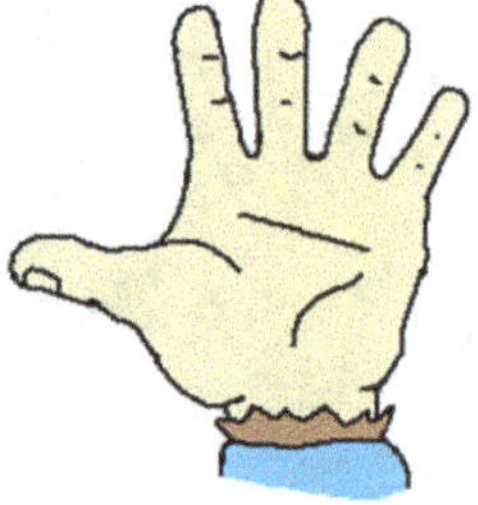

hand

king

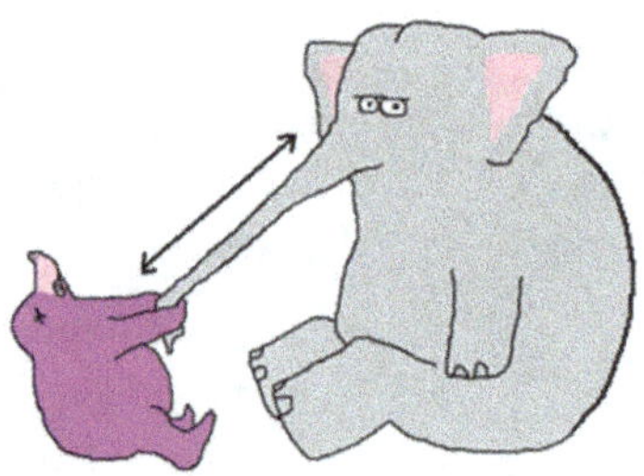

long

thing

think

melt

A Thing for the King

Made by my hands for you.

What do you think?

The nose is too long!

And it has a big bend.

The ears are too long!

The face is also too long!

This is a bad thing!

Melt it and make it again!

(Later...)
Made by my hands for you.

What do you think?

YES!! This is a good thing!

check

rich

much

phone

graph

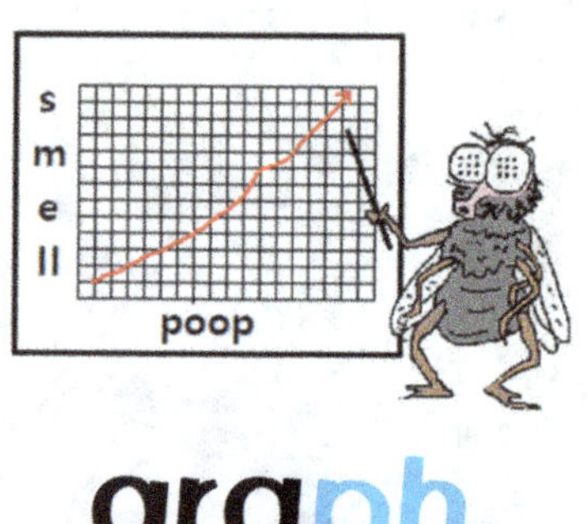

ship

cash

Rich man on his ship
How much?
How much?
Check the graph

Rich man on the phone
How much?
How much?
Check the cash!

photo

hum**ph**

shake

pu**sh**

chin

chop

whole

Chin Man
CHIN MAN

I am CHIN MAN!
CHIN MAN

I have a very big handsome chin.
CHIN MAN

Humph! Your big chin is not very handsome.
CHIN MAN

I can push a huge ship!

Humph! That ship is not huge.
CHIN MAN

I can chop a tree with just one hand!
chop!

Humph! You should not chop trees
CHIN MAN

I can shake a whole house!
shake
shake

Humph! Shake a house?! That's too much.
CHIN MAN

Also, I am very very rich.
CHIN MAN

Wow!
Yay!
Take a photo!
CHIN MAN

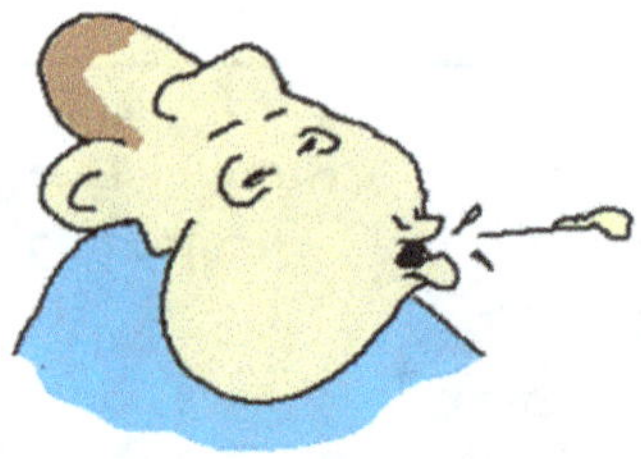

sp**it**

ga**sp**

thick

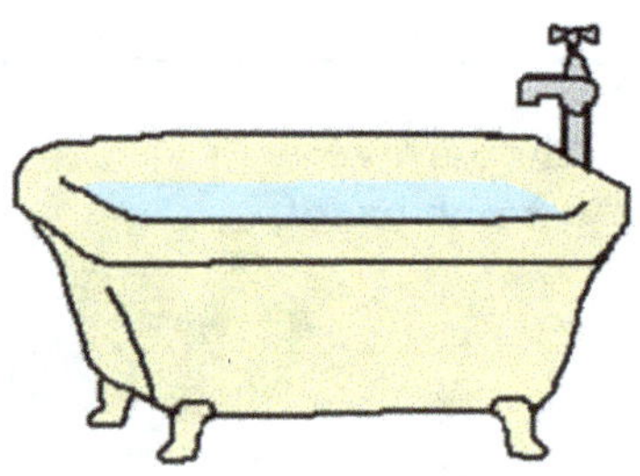

ba**th**

trash

truck

smoke

Trash truck in the thick black smoke
Trash truck in the thick black smoke
Trash truck in the thick black smoke
Choke and spit and gasp

Trash truck in the thick black smoke
Trash truck in the thick black smoke
Trash truck in the thick black smoke
I think I need a bath!

thin

moth

space

wasp

smash

smile

Space Wasp vs. Moth Man

Moth Man fixes his spaceship.

But Space Wasp can see him.

Space Wasp has a scary spaceship.

He is hunting Moth Man.

Moth Man has no time to think!

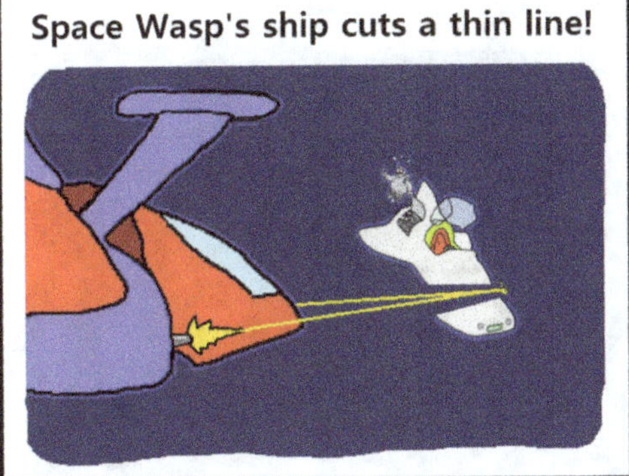

Space Wasp's ship cuts a thin line!

But the space suit is too thick.

CRASH! Moth Man is like a moth!

Space Wasp says, "I give up!"

Space Wasp's ship is smashed!

And Moth Man smiles.

Chapter 4   129

strong

fa**st**

scuba

ma**sk**

swan

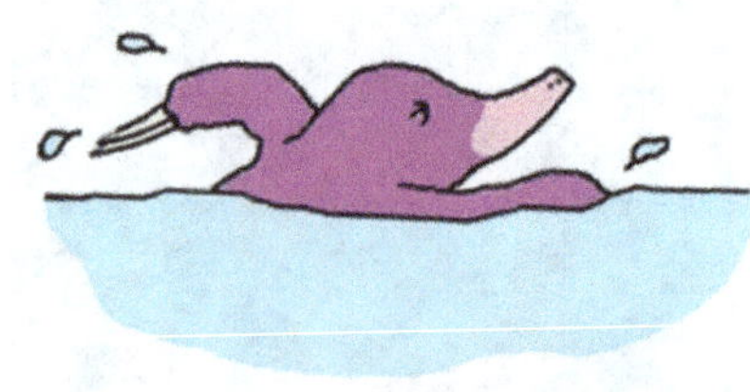

swim

snake

Snake in a scuba mask
Swimming in the sea
Strong and fast
As he can be

Swan in a scuba mask
Swimming in the sea
Strong and fast
As he can be!

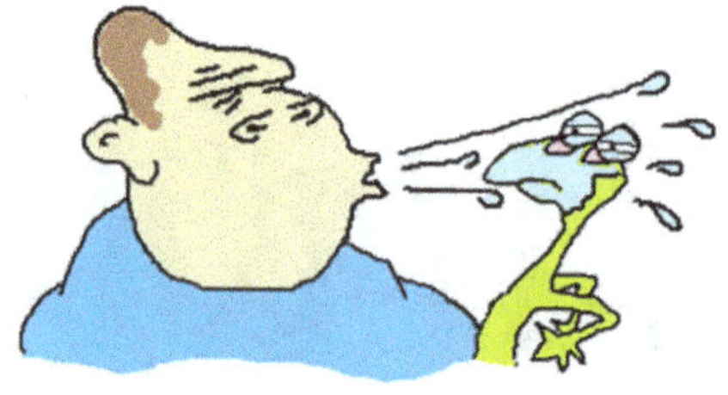

sneeze

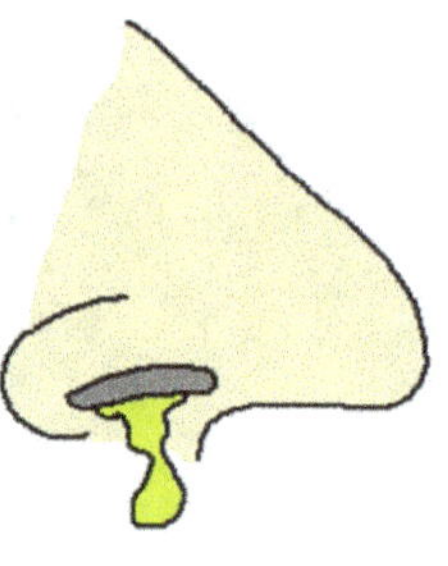

snot

stop

guest

vest

disc

It looks like snot.

Chapter 5

VOWEL COMBINATIONS

Welcome to vowel combinations!

Did you know?

Vowel sounds are not just A,E,I,O, and U! They can be made of other letters too!

Learning about those kinds of vowel sounds can seem like a super-human task!

That's because it seems
even the letters themselves
can't agree on how to
make **vowel** sounds!

We can't control them with rules.

We just have to remember each
new sound they make together.

ai ay ea ee

day

say

way

eat

meat

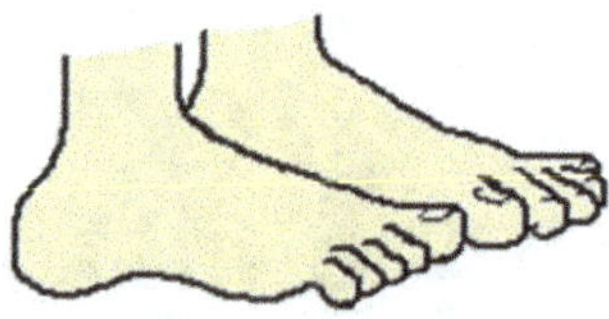

feet

I eat meat
With my feet
I do it every day

People say
"Don't eat that way"
"To eat that way is bad"
They say

But I eat meat
With my feet
I do it every day!

ai ay ea ee

sail

train

wait

play

slay

stay

clean

near

teach

creep

sleep

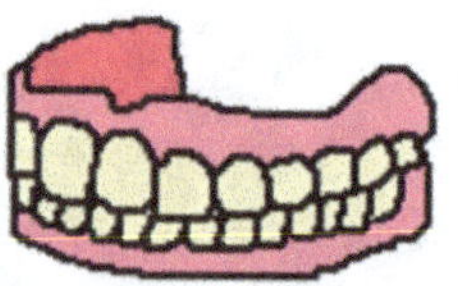

teeth

The Mean Green Dragon

oa ow oi oy

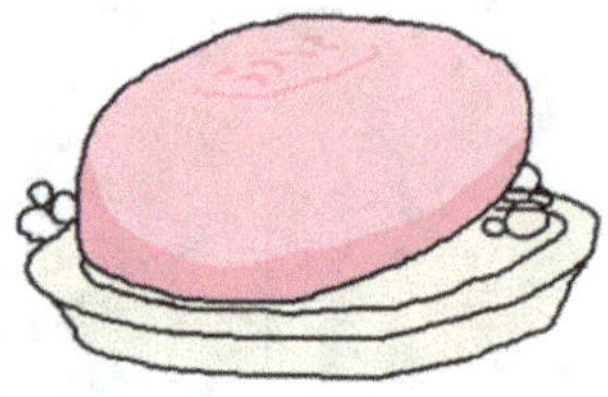

s**oa**p

thr**ow**

b**oi**l

t**oi**let

oyster

Boil oysters in a toilet
Boil oysters in a toilet
Boil oysters in a toilet
Put some soap in

Boil oysters in a toilet
Boil oysters in a toilet
Boil oysters in a toilet
Throw them in the bin!

oa ow oi oy

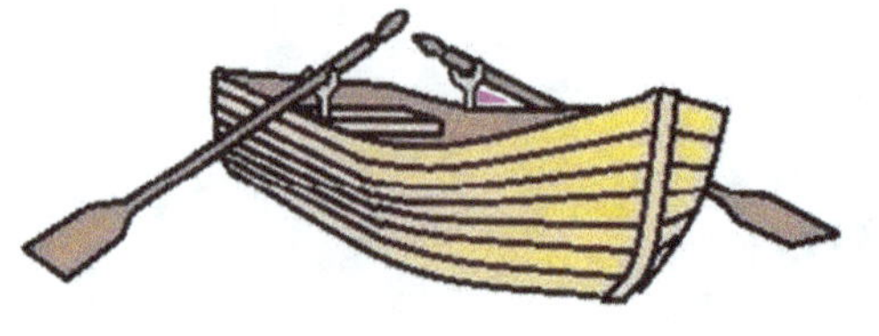

boat

coat

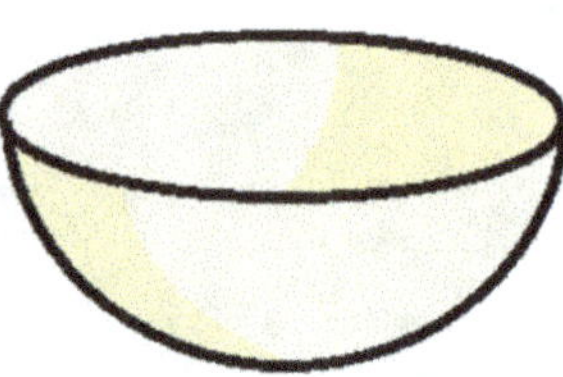

bowl

slow

noise

annoy

boy

toy

Debora Sailaway was very cute.

Deb's mom cut her hair with a bowl.

Deb liked her bowl-cut.

Deb also liked to sail toy boats.

One day she took her toy boat to the lake.

A boy there was very mean.

The boy's boat made a big noise.

And Deb's toy boat was gone!

20 years passed.

It was the same mean boy! Deb was really annoyed.

She took the boy's sword.

And the boy's hat and coat.

And the boy's big boat, too!

Chapter 5   145

ou ow ar or

house

out

cow

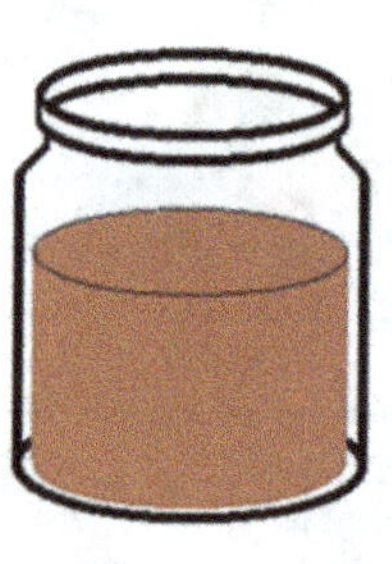

brown

car

fart

corn

Brown cows eating corn
In a car
Did you fart?
Did you fart?
Get out of the car!

Brown cows eating corn
In a house
Did you fart?
Did you fart?
Get out of the house!

ou ow ar or

mouse

shout

down

owl

guard

shark

horn

short

The Mouse Beach Guard

I will go to my house.
Now you are the guard.
Okay.

A shark or an owl will eat a mouse.

If you see a shark,
you must shout, "SHARK!"
Okay.

Every mouse will run
out of the sea.
SHARK!

If you see an owl,
you must blow this horn.
Okay.

Every mouse will run
down to the sea.

Make it a long blow,
not a short blow.
BLAAAAAAAR!
Okay.

See you tomorrow.
I'll go now.

A short time later...

Umm... if I see a short shark,
I must shout "Owl!" No, no...
OWL!

Umm... if I see a long owl, I must
blow up a short shark. No, no...

Umm... if I see a shark with horns...

HORN!   I must blow the horn!

BLAAAAAAAR!

oo oo ew ue

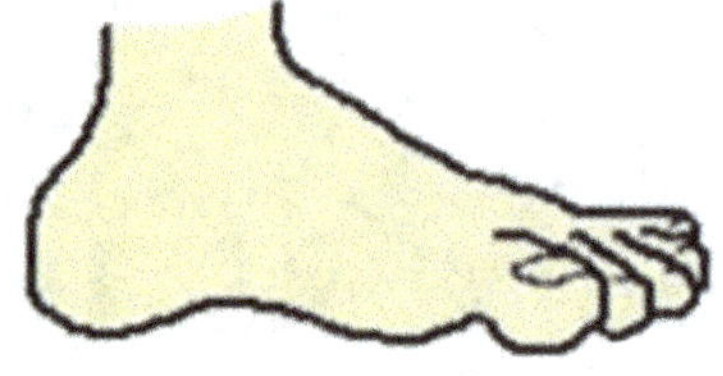

f**oo**t

f**oo**d

ch**ew**

st**ew**

bl**ue**

gl**ue**

Don't put your foot
In my food
Your foot I cannot chew

Don't put blue glue
In my stew
I cannot chew blue glue

Foot in food
Glue in stew
I cannot chew
This food from you!

oo oo ew ue

cook

wood

look

new

pool

room

snoop

spook

zoo

clue

true

I don't like our new house in this zoo.

We have to cook our food with wood.

And I don't like blue in every room.

It has a really cool pool!

But humans snoop around the pool!

Don't be spooked. The pool has a new blue gate.

Look! Who chewed the new blue pool gate?

I can make it good as new.

I will use glue.

Look! A clue!

Foot-prints from the pool...

...to the living room!

Oh Lord... is it true?

I know who chewed the new blue pool gate.

It was YOU!
Yes, it's true.
But that's what lions do!

The Story of Cool R

People say R is "bossy"
because A,E,I,O, and U
are a bit quiet around it,
but perhaps just some
of them are quiet
because they think
R is so cool.

After all, they're not always quiet next to R.
It's just in certain words!

The Story of Q and U

Did you know? Q and U are married!
Everyone at the wedding thought a *vowel* and
a *consonant* were too different to be married,
but they didn't care!

U often goes out alone,
but Q very rarely goes
anywhere without U.

When they are together,
U is silent.
They are very happy
together.

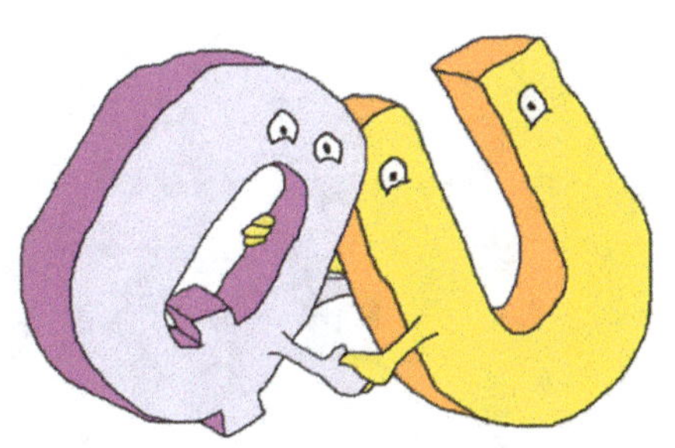

erir orur

germ

perm

dirt

worm

fur

Dirt and germs in my fur
My fur has dirt and germs

Dirt and worms in my perm
My perm has dirt and worms

Dirt and germs and fur and worms
Fur and worms and dirt and germs

Dirt and worms in my perm
Fur has dirt and germs!

Herbert   teacher   girl   stir

doctor   sailor   word   work

burp   hurt   surgery   turn

The Ship's Doctor

Herbert Burger was a good doctor.
Best Doctor 1820

He worked on a big boat.

Every day he would cure the sailors.
Next..

He could fix a broken arm.

Or wrap a hurt head.

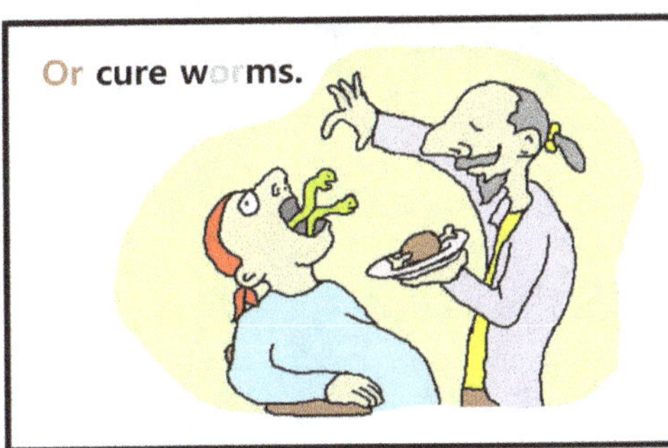

Or cure worms.

Or stir a brew to cure burps.

But his best work was surgery.

He would always heed his teacher's words.
JUST CUT IT OFF!

Herbert was very proud of his surgery.

But he didn't know much about germs.

No one knew about germs back then. Everyone was a bit dirty.

Herbert was a happy doctor.

Then one day he turned his head and saw a girl. Do you know her?

ou ou ie igh

grou**p**

sou**p**

pie

figh**t**

nigh**t**

Soup night, soup night
Group soup night
Grab some soup and join the group

Pie fight, pie fight
Group pie fight
Grab a pie and join the fight

Pies and soup and fights at night!
I like the group soup night pie fight!

you

couple

touch

young

lie

tie

right

sigh

The Happy Couple

When I saw you it was love at first sight.

And now we are a couple I want to say...

You are young and beautiful...

...and you touch my heart!
What?!

You say I touch your heart?!
Yes!

THAT'S A LIE!!

I don't touch things I don't own!

But last night I did touch the soup.

...and the pie.

Also, I did touch your best tie.

Sigh... maybe you are right.

Let's not fight.
Tonight I have a question:

Will you marry me?
!

No.

br**ea**d

br**ea**k

h**ey**

ob**ey**

Hey, hey!
You must obey!
Don't break the bread that way!

Use a knife
And slice it twice
Don't just break it
That's not nice

Hey, hey!
You must obey!
Don't break the bread that way!

ea ea ey ey

bear **d**ead **h**ead **h**ealth

ready **sw**eat **w**eapon **gr**eat

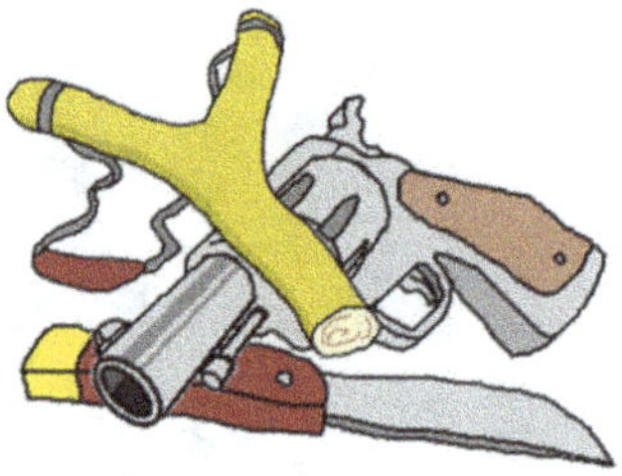

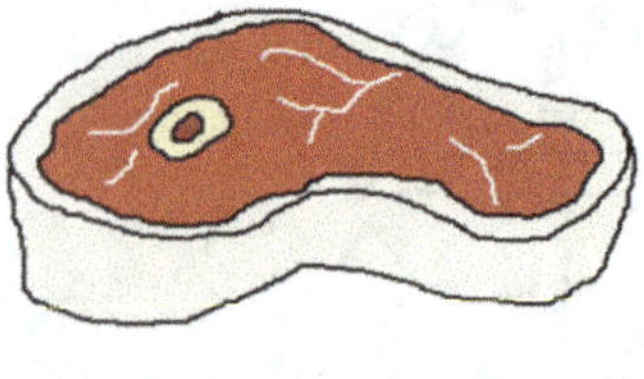

steak **pr**ey **hon**ey **mon**ey

Get ready for a great new job!

Have the key to the health club.

You need to be healthy and strong.

You must eat a lot of steak...

...and sweat a lot every day.

But I will pay you a lot of money!

This time you will hunt a wild beast!

Your prey is the great scary...

...wild, mean, huge, angry...

...honey-bee!

You will need big weapons.

Hey! This is no joke! It's deadly!

The Great Honey-Bee
has a huge head!

It's like a BEAR!

Later, in a deep valley...
sweat!
sweat!

ui oe ie ei

fruit

suit

oboe

genie

weird

Weird genie in a suit
Plays the oboe

Weird genie eating fruit
Plays the oboe

Why does he wear a suit?
Why is he eating fruit?
Why is he in a lute?

I don't know-boe!

juice

aloe

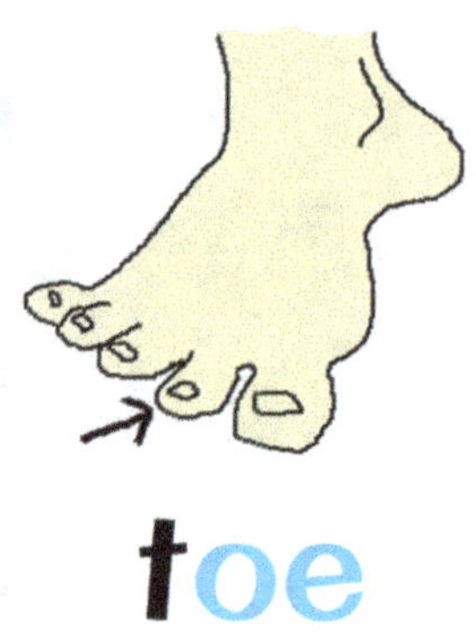

toe

thief

movie

ceiling

leisure

receive

The Doctor's Day

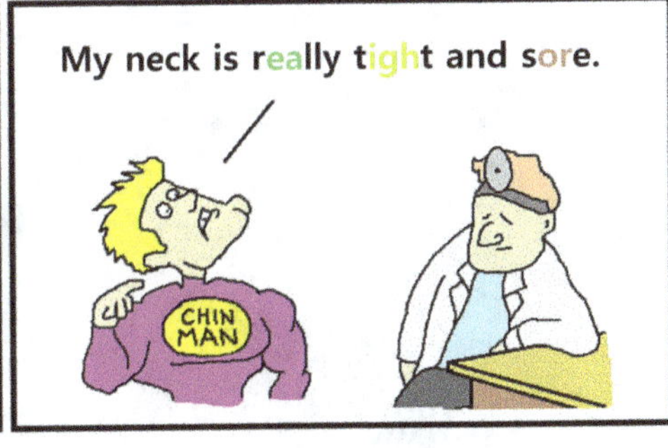

eight

t**al**k

A**u**gust

y**aw**n

I saw you talk and talk and talk
For eight days in August

You saw me yawn and yawn and yawn
For eight days in August

I saw you talk
You saw me yawn
Talk talk talk
And yawn yawn yawn

I saw you talk and talk and talk
For eight days in August

ei al au aw

veil

weight

ball

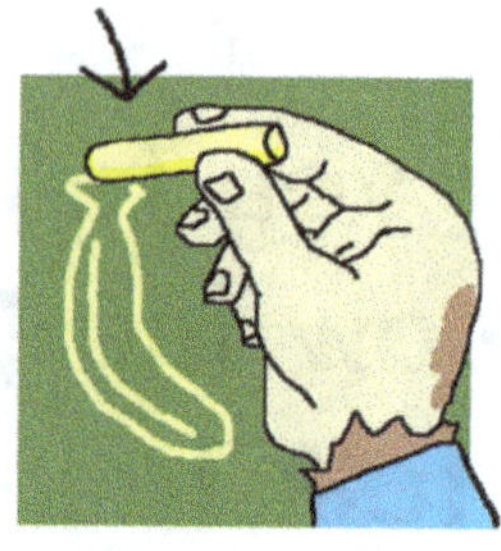
chalk

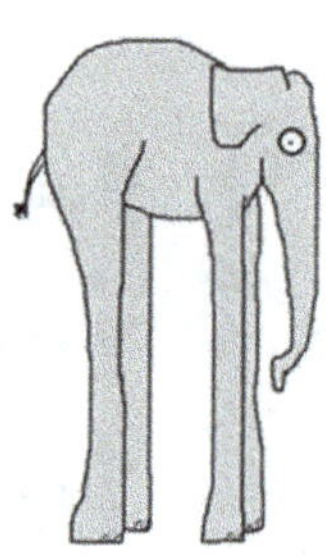
tall

fault

haul

haunt

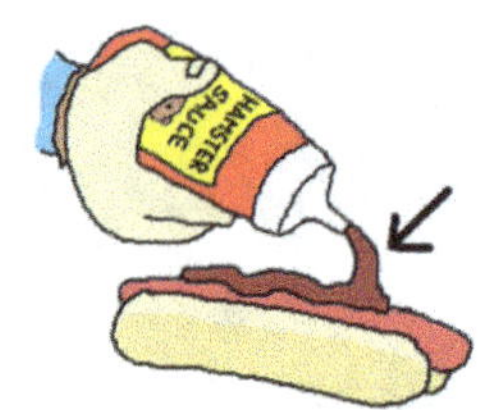
sauce

taught

awful

crawl

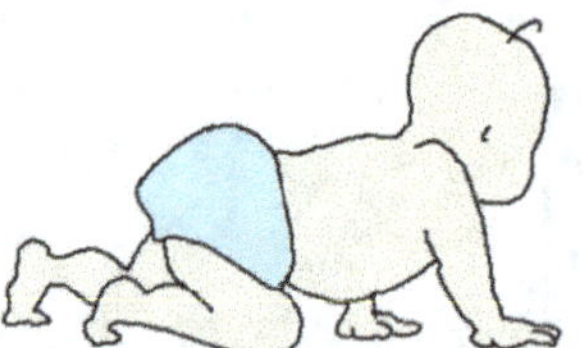
dawn

saw

The Haunted House

I am home
after eight years!

Hello, my lord.
Tomato juice for you.

Awk! This is awful!

This is SAUCE, not juice!
It's all my fault!

It's not your fault.
I taught you all you know.

Where are the ghosts?
They should haunt until dawn.

I saw the ghosts.
I was behind a veil.

I saw them talk. They were weird.

Next I saw them buy a saw.

I saw them crawl on the floor
and draw with chalk.

And I saw them saw the floor
with the saw.

...and haul a weight ball
up a tall ladder.

Ha! Is that all?
Let's talk to them.

CRASH!

THE END!

Feel free to turn the page
and have a look at our
range of phonics books.
(Just the covers.)

Phonics Series

Preschool:

  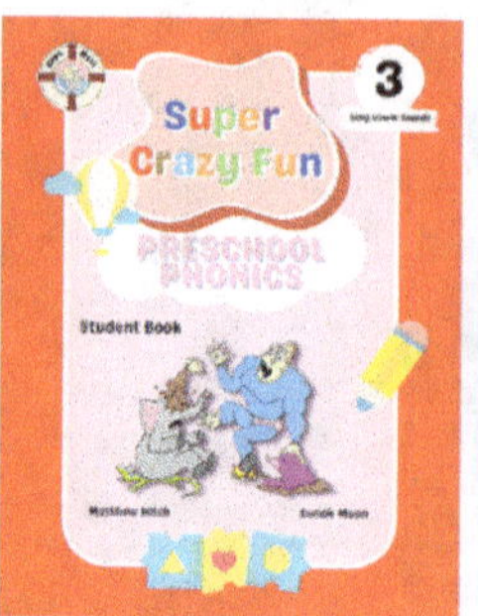  

Kindergarten:

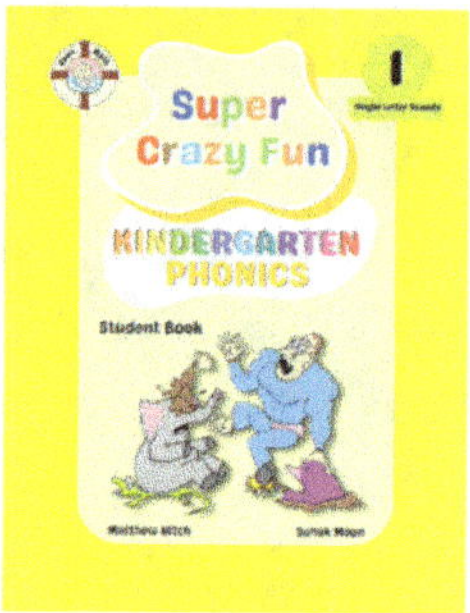    

Elementary School Junior:

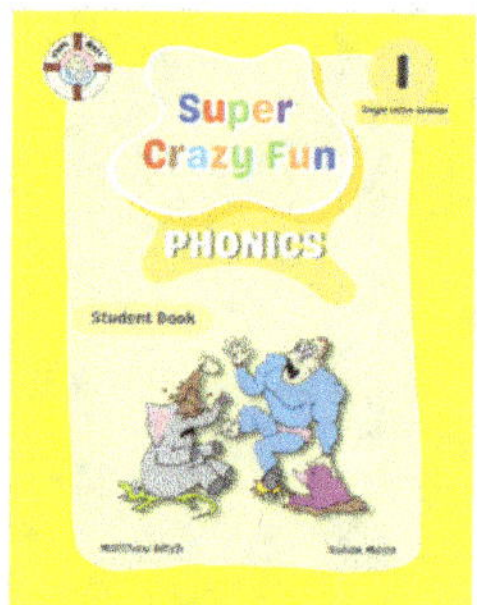 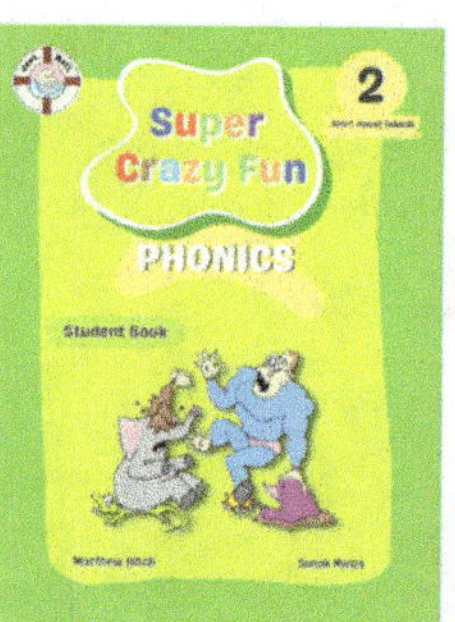 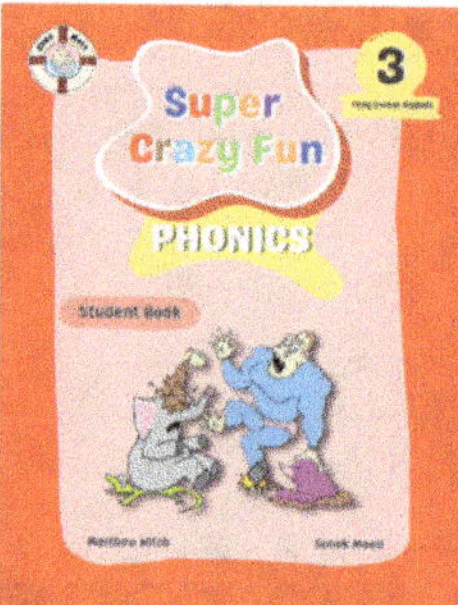  

Elementary School Senior:

See supercrazyfun.net or email info@supercrazyfun.net, or even look for Captain Matt on Amazon.com